The Musician's Companion
By: Paul Spencer Alexander

©2003, 2009 – All Rights Reserved
Paul S. Alexander
Ear Magic Productions
11012 Ventura Boulevard, #1257
Studio City, CA 91604-3546
musicianscompanion@yahoo.com
www.musicianscompanion.net

Wordclay
1663 Liberty Drive, Suite 200
Bloomington, IN 47403
www.wordclay.com

First published by Better World Publishing on 9/11/2009.

ISBN 978-0-5780-3816-2 (sc)

Printed in the United States of America.

This book is printed on acid-free paper.

For my family, and for all the children of music.

Acknowledgements:

I dedicate this book to my readers over the years. As I journey through the pressing of this latest edition of the Musician's Companion, I still find myself calling it the "official" pressing, though it has been a living, brick-and-mortar document updated over the years as the music marketplace changes. I think back and realize it only existed as an E-book ordered by a modestly-sized group of musicians who were throughtful enough to not only take my advice, but actually pay money for it, too. I sent those E-books by hand, one-at-a-time, there was no "automation" in my life then (though this book has since been rebuilt with the lesson of "automation" as its _premise_). I think about the 24-hour-or-less "E-book delivery guarantee" that I had no choice but to offer since I was not technologically equipped to provide my readers with an "instant download" set-up after purchasing. I get personal satisfaction as I look back though, realizing I "marketed my butt off" with that E-Book, and stuck to my guarantee 100% of that time period, with no complaints or nasty comments/critiques by ANY of my readers about the book. I am thankful and grateful to ALL of you. I hope the E-book helped to advance you in some way, and my prayers for your ongoing success are with you.

As I revise and revamp my intellectual and (spiritual) view of the music industry and the world around us, I update this book and create another (humble) ceremony (but a ceremony, none the less) with a hope that the words written here will spread and more and more people will want to read this. I want as many songwriters and musicians to pick this up and give it a read as possible.

Thank you again.

4

TABLE OF CONTENTS

"Which can say more than this rich praise, that you alone are you."
Shakespeare

1.) INTRODUCTION
(DO ONE THING AT A TIME & GIVE YOUR ATTENTION TO ONLY ONE PERSON AT A TIME).

The army of distractions and ominous piles of information, signs, and messages we receive in the real world and in the cyberworld are enough to make us truly mad. Even calm folks who have no such challenges often forget a simple secret to organizing reality and creating personal success. Do ONLY one thing at a time. Reach out towards and connect with ONLY one person at a time. This should be a way of life that is pathologically followed (as much as possible throughout your day) from the moment you rise out of bed in the morning to the moment your head hits the pillow that evening (Amen). You will have a better
experience growing your music career (and enhancing your life in general) if you make it a solid virtue and daily habit to take any number of ideas, projects, or required tasks you have in mind, and only do each and every single one of them, one at a time.

Multi-tasking is <u>not</u> something our brains are naturally accustomed to. Multi-tasking is a bi-product of an overfilled brain, resulting from an (astronomical) increase in the amount of information we must process daily in society today. With this said, we often have no choice but to multi-task.

While your ability to multi-task might have you believe that it is impressive to others, and that it makes you appear more productive and "smarter," (especially to your own self image), there is often a loss in quality to multi-tasked "completions." Additionally, one is forced to examine how much actual "accomplishment" during multi-tasking *ends with completion* of specific long-term goals.

It is unhealthy to multi-task and it is most often not necessary. If it becomes necessary, avoid it still, and make everyone and everything else wait. If you are multi-tasking on three things, the quality of your direct attention to each task (or worse, human being) is only 33 and a third percent. Put down the work and connect with him or her for a moment. If he or she is demanding too much of your time, find a way to articulate this in a manner that will give you enough time to work on your most important music project individually (or collectively) with no other distractions. The quality of your personal and professional relationships (with professional relationships as the main idea for the purpose of this book) will improve if they are truly one at a time. The quality of your work (as well as the implementation of a strategy for making your work pay off) will improve immeasurably if each are pursued separately, and one at a time. The footprints or evidence you leave behind during this behavior will be ones that hint at a good example for others to pick up on and follow. You will not only emerge as a successful music Artist and role model, after all. You will also emerge a Teacher.

Have a pen handy to jot down notes as you use this book. Some of my ideas might help you create more ideas. Mark this book up with a pen, post-its, a highlighter, or whatever works for you. Just make sure you take jot down some strategies contained here. I have found that the majority of books out there take the development of a music career and, instead of following a logical, "step by step" process from scratch (with the idea of simply building it "from the ground up"), they turn it into so much confusing information and unrealistic legal precautions (particularly for people who are starting out with nothing) that many Artists often don't know where to begin, or believe that the otherwise "possible" is "impossible." There are a multitude of reasons I have chosen to write this book, but you really only need a select handful of these reasons to help you get yourself off the ground when starting or advancing your music career. I have found that a "step by step" approach works best for me, and it is my hope that it will work wondrously for you too.

In order to apply the all-important virtue of doing only ONE thing at a time, you MUST be actively applying this rule DAILY by doing a minimum of ONE significant and specific thing each day to grow your music career. You need to focus on it and complete it in one day and, if you complete it and still have time that day, then do a second thing for your music career, and only focus on that second thing alone until it is also completed. If you can get ten things done, all the better, but it might make you "slag" on day two, and forget about day 3 and the days that follow. The all-important rule is (a minimum of) ONE task a day. This is something you can stick to, no matter how busy your life is.

Every effort has been made to provide resources for the promotion of your music that will "stand the test of time." At the time of this publication, all resources mentioned were fully operating on the World Wide Web. However, within the colossally over-saturated universe that "is" cyberspace, many companies and resources shut down quite a bit, as new ones continuously "pop up" out of nowhere; and ones that "pop up" out of nowhere are the ones you should be the most skeptical of. Hence, website addresses come and go, as competition is as fierce as can be during what is still the "infancy" of the Internet. If, in the event, you go to any website listed in this book, and it is out of business (which is unlikely), please know that there are comparable websites that can assist you in a similar way. The most important important thing to know when reading is that I have already attempted to sift through the pile of weeds to locate some flowers in the garden. Keep this (also) in mind when doing your own research to avoid "scammers" of any kind. PLEASE USE CAUTION WITH YOUR OWN CAREER, BECAUSE THERE IS SCUM EVERYWHERE. How's that for a rhyme? It happens to be true in many instances.

2.) LEGAL

Please understand that I cannot take ANY responsibility for any business/legal agreements (financial and/or otherwise), medical advice, spiritual/philosophical advice, or anything else you decide to pursue (including companies you decide to do business with) after reading this book. I am not being paid to mention any of the companies/organizations listed here. I am only spreading the word of their existence for your potential benefit, and any opinion I give is precisely that: opinion! My advice is not, and should not be taken, interpreted, or used as legal or medical advice of any kind. I speak quite a bit about the concept of "automation" in this book, because I believe it is the vital secret to a "successful life," and resources that might be valuable to you can be "automated" into your own life. With this in mind, PLEASE USE CAUTION AND DO THE PROPER RESEARCH before working with ANY companies in this book (or any company on the planet, for that matter), as the choice is yours and you are on your own with your decision. Please watch your pennies and use your best judgment if/when you decide to make an investment in time or money with anybody for the benefit of your music.

It is my sincere hope that you find something in this book that leads you to a higher level of success in both your career and your life in general. You deserve it because you have the talent and the guts to be an Artist.

And now, without further ado, it is my pleasure to welcome you to: "The Musician's Companion." Let's get started!

3.) HOW TO START A MUSIC CAREER ON "YOUR OWN TERMS"

If you take only but a moment to question how "big" you want to grow your music career, please keep something crucial in mind and use it as a vital source of (true) inner power as you get started; everyone around you is going to try and stop you. The better your work happens to be, the more worried (and vigilant) some will become in trying to influence the demise of your "vision" and your "dream." You will have to karate-chop your way through some of them and, since you may in fact not have a choice, you might as well enjoy the utilization of (yet another) gift by employing martial arts as a form of self-defense.

In all seriousness, it is in fact wiser to simply envision a brownish rubber wall that bounces the *Anti-success Undesirables* out of your life, and back into their own miserably boring and nauseatingly common existences. Become immune to ALL of it, literally. I realize that it is easier said than done, but do it anyway. This way, your friends and loved ones won't get hurt by the "cushiony rubber." *Never* use a brick wall. You'll feel badly, even if people who are genuinely "against you" smash into it and get themselves hurt. Again, never use a brick wall.

People will continue to try and stop you every step of the way, including that kid from your childhood whom you picked on when you were twelve years old (and which you may still feel badly about today). He/she might still wish the demise of your dreams today even though you are (perhaps) 32 now, and not 12. Still, I think it's time that "they" grew up by now, and not you. With this said, many will find your dream unrealistic, childish, and selfish. How unfortunate it is that they don't have your "gift" and your "calling." Some whom you love dearly will try to stop you, if only to "protect you;" (from what though, your personal happiness and sense of fulfillment)?

You will find success in music on your own terms, and as much by your own schedule as possible. This book will help you build your own little brick (I mean) your own little rubber music building with production, sales, and shows going on within it, and taking place outside of it. As you build your little company, you will reach out to "hold hands" with other companies to advance the exposure (and sales) of your music. You are going to look "good" to them. This book will offer suggestions as to "how," and will (likely) save you time during the process by cutting out the extra fluff and employing the KISS method (I'm not talking about the band). KISS stands for: "keep it simple, stupid." This is the most valuable lesson of all.

Some may even discriminate against you, your musical style, your message, your talent, your "uniqueness," or your general gumption and nerve. Discrimination is often a cheap and temporary hallucinogenic drug used by the enforcing party to mask unmanaged *jealousy* (believe it or not). It's ALL about maintaining your musical presence, despite it. You can still have "shame," while walking right through your adversaries, even if they think you "have no shame." They'll say anything, really. You know the truth though, and it doesn't matter what they think is the truth, because how could they possibly even *understand* what you can do?

This leads me to my next point; your finances. It has often been said that "living well is the best revenge." You are not going to think or believe you are "poor." You are going to live "richly," not unlike the music mogul you are going to become (on your own terms). This book will give you solid and little known financial advice FOR A LIFETIME that you will take advantage of as you are getting started. Why on earth would you wait until afterwards? Did somebody tell you it wasn't possible, given your chosen career path in music? You won't have to go through business school to employ my suggestions for lifetime financial security (starting immediately). You would be foolish not to take advantage of this research. It has taken years of trial and error. Do not go for all of the other "gimmick" websites not mentioned that will take your money and then disappear from the Internet within a year, while making no difference in the advancement of your music career, despite having taken your hard-earned money. Henry David Thoreau uttered the profoundly brilliant AND simple phrase: *"Simplify, Simplify."* Take this quotation to heart. If this does not work (although it should), make full use of the KISS Method mentioned earlier. Again, these resources and the advice in this book are yours to keep, but you <u>must</u> do the work yourself.

4.) A WORD ABOUT THE WEB RESOURCES LISTED HERE

You need to actually visit them! You need to familiarize yourself with them, *one at a time,* and make your OWN decisions about whether or not to use any of them. What's most important about many of the websites listed herein (along with the potential promotional value in them) is the databases of labels, promotion companies, studios, performance venues, and so many other vital things you need contained all in one place. An important "vision" I had when deciding to write this book was the desire to *create something* for musicians and songwriters that would lead them to all the resources they could ever possibly need, all in one easy place.

Nobody out there, including your family and many close friends, has your unique kind of *gift*. You are the Musician, you are the Artist, you are the songwriter, and you are the "light" that has made life bearable (and *intriguing*) for humanity throughout the ages because of the magic we witness through your creativity. Don't take your gift lightly, even if people have not heard your work just yet. You have been "chosen" to do this work. Your humility is (most likely) astounding because of the fact you are "the real deal," and not someone who wishes that you could be. You might not always praise yourself enough because of this.

The people you know are most likely aware of how talented you are, but they won't always tell you enough, especially at the times you need to be told, and some won't let you know it AT ALL. If only they knew how much of a difference it would make if they did tell you enough. But they won't, and it should not matter either way (even though it always seems to end up mattering). Sometimes, it is so very helpful to remember that you are the very best judge of your own work, because you're the one who created it. Often times, you'll experience criticism from others that will make you believe your work is not good enough. The real shame of this is that harsh criticism is often born from those who are listening to or watching the work of someone who is truly unique. Things are not always as they seem. Please keep this in mind.

Do you have people in your life whom (you think) are judging you as a failure because you dare to brave the storm of achieving your musical goals in order to show the world your truly amazing capabilities? Or are these people, perhaps, not judging you at all and, instead, you're just judging yourself while the rest of the world moves along without you, not thinking of you at all, and accomplishing things that you have no interest whatsoever in accomplishing (i.e. that big bank job or that other "dream job" at the insurance company)? They might actually, in fact, *be* judging you. There really isn't anything you can do about it, except leave them with a significantly potent little dose of *inner shock* by the unprecedented *metamorphosis* they will soon witness within you.

You will become more organized than they are, you will work *smarter* and not *harder* than they do, you will plan ahead and plan ahead yet again, and all who once criticized will want to know your secret. After all, you will feel GOOD. They will want to know why. You might not want to share with some of them why this is the case if you think they only want to take from you and will eventually turn on you. Many of the people you know who do not share your unique musical gift, yet have jobs that pay well, are still not feeling so good. All the while, you will make it all look easy when you need it to, and incredibly difficult during the times it is wiser to make it all look very hard since you have, in fact, worked so very hard. If you are in a total *slump,* remember that the rest of the world often assumes you are still *busy.* Look the part. If you are, either for a moment, or pathologically casting your *dignity* aside when you're alone with yourself and judging yourself to the core, you have probably also at some point realized you have accomplished quite a bit, and that *dignity itself* has taught you this valuable lesson. Hold onto your dignity and your sense of worth. You already know that climbing over a slump is not easy work.

There are some real jerks out there. Ignore them. You have talent and worth. You are good enough for gold (or platinum if that is your taste). No two individuals are alike, and we would all be in very big trouble if they were. All are unique, and all are

14

special. You are unique, and you are special (not to mention, unusually so). If you do not have people in your life telling you this at all then, even if it sounds a bit corny, you are hearing it now, because I am telling you the truth. Do not ever say that someone did not share this with you. But you won't ever be at your best if you do not *believe* and feel *good.* If you are reading this book, you are likely the "real deal," or at least thought so at one point before you ran into problems. You are also competent and proactive for reading this. I am not going to give up on you either, but you'll have to stay with me. I know the entire story by heart, because I have lived it.

5.) HOW TO "AUTOMATE" YOUR PHYSICAL WORLD FOR COMPLETE SUCCESS

Some of you are quite organized already, and really have it together well. Your life might be completely perfect. For those of you in this category who are still with me, please know that this book will still be just as useful for you too. You might have never even thought about some of the strategies written here (even if you are already well-established). With this said, many and most of you are probably discouraged. I hope this is not (entirely) the case for you, and if it is the case, please try to feel a microcosm of solace in the FACT you are anything but alone. There are truckloads around you, all with a unique story. Let's get you out of the boat and into a yacht (or at least a very expensive life preserver).

Perhaps you are inconsistent with your work. There is no way you can be consistent if you haven't gotten a solid grip on your emotions, feelings, and path. Do not fall for or be sucked into believing that there is really anything wrong with you. You can still have an amazingly fulfilling life of consistency with your music. You can still have a music career and happiness in all of your creative goals. You can even have it more so than many others, despite what you might be going through. You deserve it. You are an Artist. You are a *Star;* get it?

If you happen to be brewing with creativity (which is likely the case if you're reading this), and you happen to keep a very messy, disorganized environment, the chances are likely you are a creative genius anyway. A fertile imagination can do this. Research shows that a messy and disorganized personal environment, managed by a highly creative mind is often the mark of a genius. Take some pride in this. You are going to treat yourself this way, too. A creative genius deserves such treatment. I will not settle for anything less from you, and you should not either, even if your work is on a shelf covered with a blanket of dust, and even if *you* are covered with a blanket of dust. That is why washcloths were invented; to cleanse and renew to original luster.

It is usually wisest to concentrate, master, and "automate" the things that we can always control in all the areas of our creative lives, rather than even give so much as a breath of acknowledgement to the things we cannot control, or have trouble controlling at times. This book focuses on all the things in your life that you can control and "automate," and none of the things that you cannot control (notice how I have used the previous word in quotations twice), while providing as much wisdom as possible from my own experience on weathering the situations one might feel little or no control over. We do not have to "remember" to breathe. We just do it (even during times that we question whether it is a bother to breathe at all). We do not have to remember to pump blood from our hearts to every area of our bodies. We just do. Every metabolic and physiological function necessary to your earthly survival is "automated" and working at proper throttle. This is the idea I have in mind when it comes time for "automating" the immediate physical world that you personally occupy, wherever that happens to be, and getting the environment to work only for you, so that you are free to work on your musical masterpieces. When things are automated in your life, and you both inwardly dictate and outwardly verbalize your desires and commands to the universe, a once unattainable level of peace and balance can be achieved, along with concrete results if you are consistent. Creativity usually follows, which is the antidote to writer's block of any kind.

Your emotions, your feelings, your spirituality, and everything else is entirely up to you. However, we all experience times (some much more frequently than others) when it appears that this is not necessarily the case. The focus for you (and the purpose of this book) is both the design and implementation of an "Automation Plan" for your outside, physical world to free you up a bit and make your music career a more consistent path while everyone else wants to learn your secret.

As a basic example of the concept of "automation," any job that you hold which provides (the luxury of) "direct deposit" saves you the precious time of the extra days you have to wait before the check (hopefully) arrives in the mail. If you work for someone who will not mail the check, then you have to use this valuable time to make a trip to your employer's office (costing you gas money or public transportation money) and, above all, STRESS, and even if they do mail the check to you, you still have to make a trip to the bank to cash the check or deposit it yourself. This trip to the bank costs you time and money too. The time you're spending could have been used to work on that all-important musical masterpiece.

Direct deposit is automated, (usually) lightning-fast, and on-time. It works for YOU, and you do not work for IT. It also saves you when you have transportation problems to begin with. Do you get the idea? Automated deductions from phone and utility companies also work for you, saving you the price of a stamp and a trip to the mailbox. Your life is a bit easier, and slightly more convenient because of these services.

This information is only a tiny example used to give you an idea of the concept of creating "automation" in your life. I am not just talking about work checks, banking, or billing. Since this book is about improving the quality and sense of control you have towards the accomplishment of your musical goals, through the processes of automation and *simplicity*, it will assist you in "automating" your entire life in ways that are far more significant than direct deposit and automatic billing. These are examples to show you how others have made "automation" options available to you, even if you do not take advantage of them, and even if it is at a far more basic level than the "Automation of Life Mastery."

Imagine if you could automate your life in creative (and far more significant) ways that you may or may not have heard of before, but are currently not using, regardless of your knowledge of these strategies, or lack thereof. Again, most of the resources are already there, whether you choose to take advantage of them or not. As the old adage goes, "when it rains, it pours." If you have ever experienced true inconsistency in your music career (or even just your "day job") and your emotions and feelings, then you understand that the general "organization" of your physical world often appears to (faithfully) collapse around you when you are *in downtime,* particularly if your physical world is not that organized to begin with, and which might have *lead* to it.

This collapse of your physical world (which some often refer to as "Murphy's Law"), does not help your emotional state much during "down time;" and in a "compromised" emotional state, you are even less likely to pursue the clean-up in a timely manner. Again, this is all about concentrating on the things you *can* control. These unfortunate periods of discouragement that so many musicians, songwriters, and artists encounter are often the principle reasons why "automation" of one's *physical* life can serve so infinitely well, especially in this business. Tune out the rest of the world as you read.

You are both the personal manager and the business manager of your own life, and your music career. The "two" should and can be "one" if you are organized. No one else can do these things for you. Yet, when you are discouraged and inconsistent with your work, your feelings, or have just plainly lost sight of your musical mission and the road ahead of you, then you probably make a lousy personal manager and business manager at times. Do not be discouraged by this. Again, this is where the concept of "automation" returns. You will automate your physical world to carry you through your periods of discouragement and inconsistency, as inconsistency becomes more and more of a thing of the past for you. You will feel a sense of control and security you have not experienced before towards your creative work, and that so many others whom you believe are ahead of you in some way will not have at their disposal, since they won't know your secret (unless, of course, you *choose* to share it with them).

6.) HOW TO EFFECTIVELY HANDLE DOWNTIME

Another worthy name for this chapter might have been: *"The Productive Pig Pile."* If you have a pile of clothing in your bedroom closet, on your floor, in the bathroom next to the cat box, or perhaps neatly folded and placed in drawers and on hangers, there is something you need to do right away (even if it requires getting out the iron to flatten and press those piles of clothing). If you do not own an iron, or cannot afford one, then borrow one, or go to the Salvation Army or Good Will and get one. I am serious.

This is what will be referred to as "The Seven Day Rule of Appearance." You will always be a week ahead of the ballgame being played around you while you sit in VIP box seats. Before you continue reading the rest of this section, I want you to stop what you are doing and go arrange/lay out seven days of clothing for the week ahead. If you don't have seven days worth of clean clothing, then you are just minutes away from doing a load of laundry, or embarking on a trip to the local Laundromat. It does not matter what day of the week it happens to be as you read this; *just do it*. If you are not home right now, I want you to stop reading as soon as I am done explaining this, and do not continue reading until you have gotten home and laid out seven days worth of clothing; shirts, pants, jeans, shorts, skirts, dresses, underwear, socks, belts, shoes, watch, jewelry, glasses, and/or anything else that completes your dressing for the day, should be planned *(a minimum of)* seven days in advance. If you are on a dangerously low budget (or no budget) and you happen to sweat a lot AND not have a full seven days worth of clothing, do not despair. You will rewash the items that you need to rewash. Hand washing a few pairs of underwear, socks, and/or shirts and ringing them out to air dry a few days in advance will cost you nothing. You will know beforehand what you need to put on in the morning, even if you *think* you do not have a job, or a place to go.

Now, I realize that as an Artist, you dress the way you feel inspired to dress. This is precisely the way it should be for the stage, and only the stage. If you want to do this as a business, and

you have to meet with professionals who are necessary to your success in music, then you will DRESS LIKE A PROFESSIONAL. You already know (for the most part) how you want to look day-to-day, so go along with what I am saying, even if you are not entirely sure just yet. There will be no time wasted during the process.
Each day, you will put your hairbrush,
deodorant, and all grooming tools next to the current day of clothing you will wear. Once you have chosen seven days worth of clothing, you will put them in your closet, neatly folded, side by side, or on any shelf or space in your home (or your friend's home) that you have available. You will make sure that the clothing is hidden from the general environment of your daily life (within your home). I don't care if you use a cardboard box to place these items in. In other words, just as one probably does not like to leave the vacuum cleaner out in the open and in plain sight after using it, you will also find a clever place to stash your seven days worth of wardrobe, even if you have to fold and make one single pile of all seven day's worth of clothing in some type of container or chest.

There is a reason you are going to do this, and it has everything to do with shifting periods of "downtime" or deep discouragement, when apathy (might) kick in, and you are (perhaps) less likely to function or thrive on a given day towards the advancement of your musical goals, since you're feeling "badly" and your whole environment is a complete mess. You do not know where everything is, specifically your clothing that is disorganized, dirty, and/or left in piles, and you might not even care. I hope this is not the case. You are too talented and bright not to care. Not everybody is qualified (artistically) to pick up a book like this.

We are going to work on strengthening a weak muscle into top form through gentle exercise that will affect your whole physical universe (so that you can properly manage the mental part of your universe). This weak muscle goes far beyond your clothing and appearance in your physical world. You might be the type who is less likely to "deal with this day and get things going correctly and efficiently." I am one of these people myself from time to time, though less and less still. If everything regarding your appearance is laid out, neat, clean, and ready to be used that day (since you planned it in advance), you will be much more likely to get dressed and get going, even if you feel like garbage, and even if you (think) you do not have a place to be.

If you can afford to go buy a few nice things at low price, then go do it. If you know that on certain days you need to look formal while on other days you need to look casual, get EVERYTHING ready seven days in advance. Feel free to plan up to a month or more in advance (I realize that this might be unrealistic), but do it if you can. Again, taking about an hour or so to plan this will save you from one more annoying ritual as you race around trying to "find clothing" and getting it together on one particular day, at the very last minute. You will find that hugely successful executives and highly productive people also "get this edge" over the competition by laying out all clothing days and days in advance. You will have to think and behave like a highly successful executive, or you should choose another career path, and downgrade your music to a hobby (Heaven forbid). Go take care of the clothing situation now. I will wait. You should not still be reading if you have not done this yet.

7.) PRE-REQUISITE TO YOUR TWO WEEK MUSICAL ENTERPRISE

We are going to get into some very important details here about physical packaging of your complete "Act," and how to transform the "intangible" but "divine" presence of music and sound into something tangible and marketable. But first, we need to help those who are unemployed, or are having trouble paying their bills. If you ALREADY have a job, you can skip to the next section on starting your musical enterprise, or continue reading this section for any additional pointers you might need to pick up on, regardless.

Do not let any consultant tell you that you can begin making a complete living on your music alone without having a regular job. This is so unrealistic. The best idea, though, in how to weather this tough reality is to get a job at a recording studio, royalty collection company like ASCAP, BMI, or SESAC, a publishing house, or any other place (preferably involving music) that suits you. You might also make the decision to work in a place that has nothing to do with music. This is fine, too. Money is money, but music is ALL you, and not your employer's business (unless, or course, you can offer your performances or writing to them in ways that do not create a conflict-of-interest). If you want to take on a part-time, non-corporate job, you can try a website like www.snagajob.com. If you would like something more full-time or corporate, you should first go to www.careerbuilder.com, which boasts an electronic search agent, available free of charge, and which can automatically email you job prospects on a weekly basis, based on your search criteria, free of charge; think *automation* here.

If you insist on going corporate, you might be avoiding the prospect of updating your resume (that is, if you can find it), you might not even know how to write a resume, you don't know who to hire or even where to look (and you do not need anyone to do this for you anyway, despite what you might think). You also might not even own a computer or laptop. You might be too stubborn to go to the library to use a computer there, and just the thought of such an out-of-the-ordinary process might be too much to bare.

It is amazing how many people do not have jobs and do not even have a resume. I had a computer professor at college who used to tell students to avoid pre-loaded resume templates existing in such programs as Microsoft Word (and other far-less expensive programs that can do the same thing). She would complain that pre-loaded resume templates that allowed you to fill in your work experience exactly on the areas of the template pointed out for you, were somehow "bad." Nothing could be further from the truth. I have landed many jobs using pre-loaded Resume templates, and my resumes have always been immaculate. There is no need to reinvent the wheel. Your months or years of procrastinating over how to create a resume can be over in less than an hour if you take the time to focus and use a template from Microsoft Word, or any inexpensive Resume CD-ROM available at national discount office supply stores, sometimes for as little as ten dollars. You will have choices on styles and formats with (artificial) areas of work experience pre-filled as examples within them to show you how your resume will look once it is completed. You delete the sample text, simply replacing your own educational, work, and life experiences in the areas that replace these sample areas in the pre-made Resume. Nobody will know you used a program, and it is none of their business. The Microsoft Corporation came up with these wonderful resume tools to save you time. If you do choose to reinvent the wheel or can afford to throw money at the problem instead, but do not know where to turn, go to www.careerpro.com. There are also zillions of other resume services. CareerPro happens to be a national resume company, so there might be one in your local area. I used them myself when I graduated college, and they are top-notch. With this said, I probably did not even need to use a resume service, and you should probably just do the resume yourself like I eventually did, as no one will know that you used a template. The Resumes I have done using templates have been cleaner and more to the point than others I've seen done by professionals. "Cleaner" and "to the point" is a WINNING combination that should exist in any Resume. Companies reviewing resumes do not have the time to read extra "fluff," and they are only skimming most Resumes for vital qualifications and experience. If you do not own a computer, borrow one from a friend and look up the preloaded resume templates in Microsoft Word (or in an inexpensive Resume program). You will be glad you did.

Let us now talk about an automated approach to job searching, and then we will get your Music Enterprise set up as quickly as possible. First, please realize that most of the things that you need to accomplish can be accomplished very quickly online. This includes everything right down to ordering a pizza, or even ordering up a doctor. I am very serious when I suggest that you should find a way to get your hands on your own computer. Think automation here.

When it comes time for a job search, it is (once again) unnecessary to reinvent the wheel. While I do not necessarily recommend any of the national Resume-posting, job search websites (due to the huge volume of other resumes competing for your attention), you might be able to put websites like www.monster.com and www.hotjobs.com to good use if you are wise enough to simply pick up the phone and do a polite and friendly follow-up about the status of your resume on a weekly basis. Making that wise phone call is SO VERY IMPORTANT. Do not wait for them to call you, because you most likely will not hear from them at all. Again, this is due to the number of resumes competing for prospective employers' attention. With this said, public online bulletin boards like Craigslist are probably much better candidates. By simply making the decision to PICK UP THE PHONE to speak with someone about the specific position you have applied for, letting them know you have sent a Resume and are wondering if anyone has had a chance to review it, despite their busy schedules (be sure to mention what that position *is*), you will be doing something that sets you apart from thousands of other job applicants. Most of your competition (in the form of other peoples' Resumes) will never have a voice followed by a face attached to them for the simple reason that they did not make a friendly phone call at all, did not do follow-up on the resume they submitted, and if they did do a follow-up of any kind, they did it through email. Email, in my opinion, is less-than-satisfactory as a form of follow-up, particularly with a large company, and should only be used as a supplement that will thank the person who assisted you over the phone regarding your inquiry. They are going to have to work with you, and they are definitely going to want to know what your personality is like; make sure your personality is friendly, cooperative, intelligent, and easy-going. Most if not all of the companies that list jobs on these large websites will not "ask you" to call them. Some might not even leave a phone number. Unless you are a musician seeking performance work through an agency that blares the words: "No phone calls," I would highly encourage you to simply look up the phone number of the company yourself, even if they do not list it on the job site, and give them a friendly phone call.

You really should get a computer (or better yet a laptop, which is all I use). If you go to www.recycler.com, www.craigslist.org, www.ebay.com, or browse through a Pennysaver, Thrifty Nickel, or any other publication that allows regular folks to sell used goods, there are individual private sellers who (often) sell their laptops for as little as $100.00, either just to get rid of them because they got something newer, or simply because it has an "outdated" version of Windows. If you are low on funds, in a crisis, or just want to get your life together <u>fast</u>, please keep in mind that (even) older computers still have brilliant word-processing capabilities and are Internet-capable. The older versions of Microsoft Word can still toss up a beautiful resume for you in no time. Microsoft Works (or in some computers, another program called "Lotus") usually comes pre-installed, while Microsoft Office costs extra. These two pre-installed programs (or any inexpensive word processing program) will also (usually) make a Resume. Once it is printed out on paper, you won't know which program made the Resume. If you can afford a new computer then buy one. This is, of course, preferred. If not, buy an older piece of (fill in the blank) and accomplish the exact same thing you need to accomplish anyway. You will probably end up with more money down the road as a result of the work you do on this computer, and you will likely be able to purchase a brand new model shortly down the road.

Do not let gadget-savvy posers stick their noses up at you or deter you from your core requirements of self-improvement and musical growth. Think about the classic tale about the tortoise and the hare. Block all these people out, and just get yourself going. If you are broke, then you do not have a choice. The technological oldies that society often passes up are often still goodies, particularly if you happen to be desperate. Just keep your approach simple. The goal is to get you out of a slump. The goal is to get you a job if you need one.

With all this said about job searches, you will probably do even better by using an online version of ANY major newspaper for the city you happen to live in. Do not go scrounging around and/or spending money on big, bulky newspapers that make your fingerprints black, as well as your coffee mug, and you or your "caretaker's" furniture. If you are in a city like Los Angeles, the L.A. Times Job Search area of their website is FREE, is meticulously categorized, and most importantly, is localized (as opposed to those hugely competitive national job search websites). If you are in Boston, you would check www.boston.com or The Boston Globe Online Edition. If you are in New York, you would use The New York Times Online, and if you are in ANY other city in the entire country, just use the online version of your local city newspaper's Help Wanted section, or Craigslist (mentioned earlier), which is INTERNATIONAL. Your Resume can quickly be sent electronically, saving you money and time. Again, you will do lots of polite follow-up, OVER THE PHONE, on a weekly basis, sending a supplementary email to the person on the other end of the phone who was courteous enough to help you with your inquiry. You can accomplish everything I have just mentioned without even leaving your home, even if your environment is a real mess. At least you will still have your coffee with you, even if you are not clean-shaven.

I am a firm believer in the basic goodness of all people. If you are in a slump, I believe it is perfectly okay to let people know, as long as you use your discretion. If you are looking for a new job, networking with friends, family, and anyone else you meet can be the very best way to start a whole new positive chapter for you. Social networking sites like www.facebook.com and www.twitter.com can help with a job search, in addition to the ENORMOUS potential of exposure you can get for your music through social networking (more about that later). Let everybody know you are looking for work, and that you have a Resume. If you are on the rebound and you know this person personally, it is perfectly okay to let him or her know you are on the rebound. Find the words that you believe in your heart of hearts are appropriate for the situation at hand. I have landed jobs in the past by telling people I have met personally the truth about my own life and circumstances. You should too. Obviously, the only time you would not tell people anything negative about your life would be when you were applying for a job through one of the national or online local city newspapers, and making your friendly follow-up phone call. You only get "personal" when you meet people personally outside of the workplace; where you meet them is up to you. You have the whole world outside your door to meet people and tell them your story. Your NEIGHBOR, who works at a company that is looking for employees might, however, appreciate your warm and honest account of your situation. I have used this strategy to land a job, and you can too.

One final (and crucial) piece of advice regarding employment; often times, it really is in your best interest to get a retail or restaurant job full-time, or any other job where the company understands that you are doing other things. Substitute teaching is one such option. Often, it is better to take the kind of job that has a high "turnaround rate" to begin with, so that when you quit the job (and begin to see your full name "in lights,") there will be no problems with this employer.

If you are dealing with big corporations and have a Resume for a "career," you might have to specify part-time instead of full-time, as most companies want you to make your career with them your life "for the long haul," since you are an investment to them. They do not want to hear of ANY "creative career pursuits" (which for you is music). Taking something corporate "part-time" (which might not be easy to get), will free up your own time and also give the correct, upfront, and above all, HONEST impression that you pursue other things. You do not want to get a job with a big company full-time, leaving them with the impression you are in it "for the long haul" if you are only thinking about a year or two. It is not the correct thing to do, and you do not know if there will be tension or a future problem if you were to look for work at a large corporation in the future. Over all, the smartest thing to do in order to save you time when looking for work at an online job website (particularly from the job search section of an online version of a major newspaper) is to type the phrase "part time" into the search phrase box, so that only "part time" jobs reveal themselves.

8.) YOUR TWO WEEK MUSICAL ENTERPRISE

Now, let's get to the goodies. We are going to get you up and running with your Musical Enterprise, and we are going to practice the virtue of "automation" here. First things first: you need a product, and this product, simply enough, is a CD. Do not get yourself crazy about how long a full-length album should be, as EP's are okay as well (which just contain a few or more songs). We are not going to think in terms of the word "demo" here. A demo properly packaged is an EP (or album) to begin with, and we are not going to "shop it to industry" in the way you might imagine. As we travel further into this, please realize that, just like the concept of a pre-loaded template Resume, no one will EVER know what methods or strategies you used to create your recorded musical masterpiece once it is done. Again, it is none of their business. A musical track you think is a demo, can be regarded as finished if it is "clean" and well-packaged, even if it is done at home on a four track. Yes, everybody loves Protools, as it is the industry standard throughout the recording industry. But if you do

not have Protools, or you are listening to one of those techie-posers

I mentioned earlier that has "the best of everything," you are wasting your time. They will steal your energy if you do not have the digital goods to compete with them. Thankfully, you have a lot more musical talent than they do, right? You do not need Protools right now unless, of course, you want to purchase it along with a computer that is powerful enough to run it, or you want to spend the money and go into a studio to record your tracks (which is fine, but you really do not need to). Please keep in mind that most, if not all of the "national" discount office supply stores sell excellent software for recording music on your computer, and many of them are around $50.00 or so. These software programs are "virtual" recording studios, just like Protools, that can get the job done right, even if you are on a budget. "Mixpad," a simple and GREAT laptop or land computer recording console, is available for instant download at: http://www.nch.com.au/mixpad/index.html. It is actually "free" to use for a period of time, but only costs around $50.00. NCH also has tons of other useful software for a huge range of digital media.

When I first started recording songs professionally (and no longer going to an outside studio to record the music), I would record all the music myself in a home studio, taking the finished musical tracks to a studio and recording just the vocals there. I would leave it to an Engineer to mix my vocals and, overall, this was not a bad strategy. Now, as it turns out, I often do my own vocals at my studio, eliminating the need of having to pay an outside source for any production work. What I just mentioned about doing all the music yourself and cutting your vocals at a studio is really quite a decent strategy (particularly in terms of significantly reducing productions costs). But you can cut your own vocals too. Keep in mind that most Artists and bands make a huge critical error during the recording process by downgrading their vocals as the very least of importance, focusing 90% of their

time on the music, and taking only about an hour or so to do the vocals. This is oh-so-very foolish, indeed. The reason Artists and bands make this mistake is often because they are booking (roughly) a ten hour block of outside studio time at an expensive hourly rate and, because of this, they have no choice but to save their vocals for last, while spending the majority of their precious studio time polishing up and layering their instrumental tracks.
This leaves little to no time left for those (sacred) vocal harmonies of yours, which could be a lot more developed if you had more time!

Your vocals are the very most important part of your production unless, of course, you're doing instrumentals, OR you are a songwriter who only wants to market your songs to *other* singers or bands (preferably by working to get a publishing deal with a reputable publishing company). If you *are* the singer or band, spend as much time with your vocals as you can, getting them exactly the way you want them. Make sure your vocals are crisp and "up front." You can do this in a home studio through lots of mixing "trial and error." Or, if you prefer, you can throw money at the problem instead by going to a studio.

If you have a four track and a computer or laptop (even if it's the cheapest computer or laptop imaginable), here is a trick: You record your music and vocals onto your four track recorder, and bounce (or ping-pong) your instruments back and forth (as you might already know how to do) so that you can layer tracks infinitely. The real trick involved during emergencies if you happen to find that you haven't bounced tracks correctly or run out of space from doubling up too many important lead instruments, is to take all that hard work and run a cord from the mixer into your computer or laptop's microphone jack, recording the music into a

wave editor program on your computer, and saving the file as a wave. I recommend Nero Wave Editor, which you can download very inexpensively online, and even get the trial version free for 30 days. You record the music from the 4 track you have run out of room on into the wave editor, save it as a wave file, and then record the entire production back onto your 4 track (but onto a single track). You've just created 3 or more tracks for additional instruments, vocals, and harmonies. Check the levels carefully when you record from your 4 track to your computer, and then back again.

The beauty of Nero Wave Editor is that it is part of a complete program called Nero Burning Rom. When you are done recording your song and vocals on your four track, you can record them into Nero Wave Editor, adjust levels, add effects, and then burn a CD using Nero Burning ROM. If you have a "dinosaur" of a laptop computer or tower, and it doesn't have a CD burner, go out and buy an inexpensive, external CD burner at a discount office supply store. Also, if you have older songs that are sitting on the shelf collecting dust, but you only have them on tape or CD (WITHOUT the individual tracks stored in a format where each track can be separated again into a mixing board for additional music and vocal layering), AND you have been putting off (perhaps for years) the daunting task of even dealing with those songs because you think that there aren't enough instruments, the track is too "thin," it's too much of a "skeleton version" that doesn't show your true potential, you're too much of a perfectionist, or blah, blah, blah, you might want to think about taking that GREAT song that's on tape or CD and running it onto a single (or double) track in a mixer (through the "line out" or "headphone jack" of a CD player or tape player), adjusting the levels, copying it to a second track on the mixer for a "richer, more full-bodied sound" (since it might be clear, crisp, but not technically "in stereo"), and THEN adding on some more

music and vocal harmonies onto your mixer. Once you're done

doing this, take your NEW AND IMPROVED masterpiece of a song that you've successfully brought back from the dead, run a cord back into your computer or laptop, record it into Nero Wave Editor, add your effects, adjust the levels, burn a CD using Nero Burning ROM, and THEN release your "Divine Resurrection of a Song" to the world.

You can save all your music as Wave files (data files) for future use, and you can also convert them as a separate file into an MP3, also using Nero Wave Editor (change the name of the file a bit when you're saving by adding "MP3" to the end, and choosing "MP3" from the drop-down menu as a saving format). Voila! Now you're ready for Apple itunes and all the other digital music distributors as well (which we'll work to get you into in just a little bit).

Before we move on, here is an important tip about mastering your CD. If you don't have enough money in your budget, then don't do bother with mastering your project. It's not enough of an excuse for choosing not to release your music. The only thing you really should take great care in is that the levels to ALL the songs are "even" with one another, are solid, and "crisp." Again, the levels shouldn't be too low, the levels shouldn't be too high, and all the levels to all the songs must be even. If you have to have an Engineer set the levels for you, then bring in your finished tracks to an Engineer at a studio, do it yourself, or have someone more skilled do it. Even if you do have to pay an Engineer to fix the levels for you, it is still far cheaper than a mastering job, especially when you have bills to pay and you also HAVE TO eat! Most regular folks cannot tell the difference between a recording that has been mastered from one that hasn't been mastered if the recording is WELL DONE. You just don't need to worry about it right now.

It's all about recording the songs, and doing a clean and clear recording that is LINEAR. If you have the budget for mastering, then go for it, but make sure you get somebody GOOD who is not using a cheap program to do it, and that you are not getting overcharged. The differences in pricing for mastering are astronomical, to say the least. A brilliant mastering job is usually very expensive, NOT done with a software program, and is instead "carefully done by hand" on a computer screen by a highly trained and skilled *physicist of a sound wizard* who spends hours and hours mastering your project. Again, don't let somebody who knows nothing about sound charge you thousands of dollars to do a mastering job on a cheap software program that does it in a matter of minutes. You might even want to think about finding an inexpensive mastering program at a music store (or even a national discount office supply store) if you're insistent on mastering and want to do it yourself. Truthfully, I wouldn't even bother with buying such a program, and your computer might already have one pre-installed, unless you own a "dinosaur."

One more thing about discount office supply stores that you might not be aware of, but is VERY important; many musicians go to them to buy a stack of blank CD-R's to record some copies of their music on. Great! However, the biggest mistake you can make is spending much more money than you need to on 50 (or so) CD-R's that are made "especially" for music, as opposed to 50 (or so) CD-R's that are designated for storing data, and are therefore much cheaper. Buy the ones for data instead, even though you're using it to burn a music CD. There's no difference whatsoever, so save your money. Just make sure that you keep your CD-R's well-protected and always in a case. Unlike CD's and DVD's from your favorite Artists, CD-R's tend to "flake off" and "become unusable" VERY QUICKLY if they are not protected, or are scratched (regardless of whether they were made for data or music in the first place). Both are UNLIKE pre-recorded CD's and DVD's that (often) last for decades, even if you've treated them like garbage, and even if they are significantly scratched.

You now have your songs recorded. You'd better give yourself a huge pat on the back! I'll bet you were able to get everything done in far less time than you thought you would. Right? Now you're really on a role. If you haven't recorded your songs, that's fine. The only thing I ask is that you stop reading and go do it now. This book will be waiting here when you get back.

9.) LAUNCHING YOUR LABEL, THEN LUNCH (plus the "easy" copyright formula).

You are going to start your own Independent label to "present" your CD and "Act" professionally. Don't let the false idea that this is something too complicated to do scare you. It's really quite simple, and you can get it done in very little time. Let's go through some simple steps, and you'll be up and running in no time. It will also cost you (almost) nothing to get everything started.

We are going to start by copyrighting the recorded song(s), EP, or full-length album you have just completed. If you have everything ready, feel some excitement (you deserve it), and let's get started. You must copyright your work first (and protect yourself from intellectual property theft, which is an obscure but common sort of a crime, and is also something that has been known to occur "by accident," curiously enough). Protect yourself, in three EASY steps.

(Copyright *formula*: Form SR + Form PA = "Only 1 Form now, Form CO, so don't stress").

1.) Go to the website address:
http://www.copyright.gov/forms/. Copyrighting your music, lyrics, and performances used to be covered by two separate forms: Forms SR (sound recording) and Form PA (performing arts). These two (obsolete) forms have merged as one to form a single (new) form, titled: Form CO, to replace them both. The good news is that you don't have to file separate filing fees for each of the separate "old" forms (which were 35-dollars each). Do not use the "poor man's copyright" method of sealing up your CD inside an envelope and mailing it to yourself, with the date on the processed envelope as your "proof of creation date." If you're in absolute desperation and you can't afford the 45-dollar filing fee, then go ahead if it's all you can do, but I do think you'll figure out a way because your music is too important to risk, and there (still likely) are no court cases on record where a "poor man's copyright" was furnished as "proof of any kind."

2.) Download Form CO from the copyright URL mentioned, fill it out online, and upload your music in MP3 or WAV formats (which are just two choices among a multitude of formats accepted for uploading to the copyright office, along with formats for movies and videos, manuscripts, etc). You can also print out the form, write a check or money order, and mail it in (utilizing some type of delivery confirmation) along with a physical media unit (generally a CD), but you'll have to read the instructions from the copyright office regarding the type of box you'll have to use for security reasons. Then there is the waiting game. UPLOADING instead is faster. You don't know how lucky you are! It wasn't until recently that you could do any of this online without having to get out of your bathrobe and make a tedious, needless, costly trip to the post office.

3.)   Fill out Form CO and do not file separate forms and pay multiple fees for individual songs (some still may not know this). Regardless of whether you have 3 songs or 13, have a title you intend to keep for the "body of the work" (all those songs together), file ALL songs on the one form (you will shortly be selling this "body of work" as an EP or full-length album), upload your songs along with the fee, and all should be "fine" regarding your protection from intellectual property theft (at least for now). For the sake of being thorough here, if you only have one song that you intend on having "stand alond" as a single, then go ahead and copyright it separately. Above all, you should *immediately be* completing this task right now to protect your recording career and "peace of mind."

The next thing you should do after copyrighting your music is actually the one thing that's most enjoyable, yet requires some creative thought (which shouldn't be a problem at all for you). You're going to choose a name for your new record label. You are going to think of a name you can be proud of. In fact, you're going to think of 3-5 possibilities (in order of your preferences) just in case the name has been taken.

Once you've chosen your favorite names (and I do hope you get the exact name you want), you're going to go online and visit The United States Patent & Trademark office at: www.uspto.gov. Once you get to the main page of the website at this address, click on the word "Trademarks." A list of options will appear below the "icon" when you click on it. Next, click on "Search TM Database (TESS)." This will take you to a new screen. Click the option at the top of the various choices, called: "New User Form Search (Basic)." Type in the full name you have in mind for your record label (i.e. ABC Records). Before you click "Submit Query," make sure the 2 drop down arrows are set to include "ALL" types of companies, and "ALL search terms" within the phrase. Then click: "Submit Query."

If you're lucky, no search terms will come up that are registered with a trademark or logo for that name. Or, a list will show up with various words and phrases that the database picked up on and displayed. These are various trademark names that were previously registered. They are classified as either "alive" or "dead." If the same name you've chosen is "alive," then it means you should choose a different name for your record label. If the same name, or a similar name is listed but classified as "dead," you can still go ahead and use the name. DO NOT worry about getting a trademark for your Act yet. You can worry about that when you "grow." Just do a quick Internet search to make sure there isn't a band in a different city operating under the same name or label. Above all, DO NOT hire an attorney to do a trademark search for you! He/she will likely follow the same method I just gave you, with a couple of other advanced options on the website that you can also do yourself, but which will most likely reveal the same search results as with the basic search.

You will also get a logo done for your new record label. This is the exciting part! There are logos that look like two thousand dollar jobs that people pay fifty dollars for. There are also logos that look like they cost fifty dollars, but had a two thousand dollar price tag. Don't pay a lot for your business logo. Type the phrase: "business logo" into yahoo or google and see for yourself. Again, DO NOT pay a lot for a logo, and do not go running to an Art School to find a starving student when you can get one for cheap in far less time. The EASIEST way to do this is to go to: www.aaa-logo.com. You can download their logo software program for very little money, and have a zillion options to choose from. You can create your logo in minutes.

You're going to take a short trip down to the local town hall once you're (reasonably) sure that the record label name is yours to use. There are two things you'll need to do to make this all official. You will need to apply for a business license, and you will need to file a DBA (which stands for "Doing business as"). A DBA is a business' way of letting the public know they intend to use this name, and it gives the public a period of time to declare if someone is already using it. Many Town Halls have a computer you can use to do your own DBA search for companies sharing your name and/or selling a similar product or service. Once you're reasonably sure no one else is using it, you'll call any local newspaper in your area and tell them you would like to file a DBA. The newspaper goes ahead and publishes the name of your company, and your intent to use it. The general law requires that this newspaper ad (which is essentially all a DBA really is) be published for a certain number of weeks. Once that time has passed and no one has claimed pre-existing and CURRENT use of the name, you are "in the clear" for 5 years, before you must file another one to "renew."

One thing you might strongly want to consider doing (if your home is your current "studio" or "office") is to get a Post Office Box for your Independent Label BEFORE you obtain a business license and file a DBA. Having an office address or Post Office box that is different from your residence looks much more professional and, above all, protects your privacy.

One more thing; if your home phone number and voicemail are the same as your business phone number, make sure you ALWAYS answer the phone professionally AND that your outgoing message on your voicemail is also professional. You are now in business, preferably during business hours (as well as later when necessary). It also doesn't matter what you happen to be doing in your home when you receive a phone call. The industry doesn't even need to know that you run your business out of your home, and probably shouldn't. If the television is running or the vacuum cleaner is running, turn any of these things off BEFORE answering the phone. If you're dripping wet from going jogging, you should still sound like an Executive who has been working at a desk. Are you not sure what to say when the phone rings? Try "Hello, can I help you?" or something similar. Or, answer by saying the word "Production" and NOTHING else. I like this *better*.

10.) HOW TO EASILY SET UP YOUR MUSIC WEBSITE

You have just finished burning your "Master" CD, all the levels are even, your vocals are perfect and "up front." Everything is going precisely as planned. Choose a title for your album or EP you are truly happy with, that inspires you, has cadence, and that will inspire others. We are NOT going to manufacture the CD yet if you do not have your own website. Let's talk about your website for a moment, especially if you already have one.

If you are on a tight budget, but want a professional-looking design, you can use a do-it-yourself website company like www.homestead.com. This company has been around since 1998, and has now incorporated hundreds of professional templates (many with Flash animation, which is normally VERY expensive if you start with a professional designer from scratch), hosting is included for a reasonable yearly fee, and there are many pre-made designs you can PERSONALIZE and that are GREAT for musicians and songwriters. You also get an unlimited number of websites to build within your account (so think *PRODUCTS* here)! Everything, including sound files, can be published <u>instantly</u> online from you home computer, which makes (otherwise) costly updates cost NOTHING at all. There are many other companies that offer do-it-yourself design and hosting "as one." Most of them (including Homestead) will even find someone to build the site for you if you prefer, although it is very easy for someone with little or no website design experience to build it themselves.

With all this said about do-it-yourself website building, as opposed to hiring a professional web designer, please also keep in mind the fact that most do-it-yourself website companies utilize a technology known as URL frames, which also utilizes the use of templates. There are many people who make the choice not to use these types of technologies for their own websites because these technologies are "older" and optimization and the ability to add certain technological elements to your site in the future might be a concern. Please also keep in mind that, if you decide to hire a professional designer down the road and move your website from a do-it-yourself company, you cannot move the actual site because the software and the hosting are "in one." Therefore, you have to rebuild the website and all the work you've put into it. You can always save all your text and your (own) pictures from your do-it-yourself website onto a CD-ROM (before switching hosting services) and have a designer build the website with them before you tear down the old one. You've still got all your own "work." In the meantime, do-it-yourself website companies are always an option.

Not unlike the concept of a pre-loaded Resume template mentioned earlier, just about ALL of the website design work has been done for you. There are areas on the templates where you simply type in the information about your band where it is designated for you. These areas are temporarily filled in with sample text for you to replace with your own. Each template will tell you where to put the information. Again, some of the Homestead templates are pre-customized for musicians, and include a complete set-up for albums, live shows, etc. You can also upload your own photos, post a YouTube video (which, for you, would ideally be a music video or "edited" live show), and ALL should be as PROFESSIONAL as possible. Make sure there are GOOD pictures of you, and that you look like a "polished Act." So many Artists and bands use horrible photographs, which can be likened to packaging an anniversary diamond ring in newspaper to give to your loved one. There is absolutely no need to hire an expensive photographer. Go to www.craigslist.org and find a photographer who is looking for exposure, and projects to do for free. Post an ad. Just be VERY careful when screening for a photographer, since lunatics populate a portion of this planet. Again, make sure you screen prospective photographers carefully, and do NOT meet them at their homes (or at yours). If you are a songwriter, a single, professional, and above all, "sharp" photograph will do just fine. Accent this photograph (if you prefer) with a layering of a musical instrument picture(s) or sheet music to stylize your page. There are also many other companies offering this type of format for musicians, and many of them specialize ONLY in working with musicians (so you can still do a bit more research on this topic if you choose).

The very most important reasons for having a music website are to generate online sales for your album(s); this is really #1 in importance, along with giving information on your live shows, directions to the shows, sales of tickets (preferably) *directly through* your website, a Newsletter for your Act, and an email list generator for building your fan base. All of these extras are ALSO #1 in importance (go figure). The music industry judges you based on how many CD units and MP3 digital downloads you've sold; not on how many times you're performing live. Keep these things in mind. We will get your CD manufactured and your MP3's ready for digital sales (including ringtones) in just a little bit. If you don't care to be involved in the Music Business, then just go ahead and perform, but you really shouldn't be doing any of this or reading this if you do not want to get paid for your precious talent, and do not want to "preserve" your work for others to have for a lifetime (and beyond).

Above all, your website should be continuously updated for the MEDIA and the public, so ALL Media Promoters, Writers, television shows, publishing companies, fans, and everyone else not mentioned here will see you as a WORKING Act, ALL OF THE TIME.

You should also start a "blog." Wordpress.org is the "industry-standard" for blog publishing, so go there FIRST, since they have a free blog program available (as well as paid options). A blog is an ongoing, comment forum where people can engage in an ongoing conversation by posting responses to each other's comments about your Act. It's like an online magazine that is ever-growing on behalf of your Act. You can also post news and stories yourself, and you should be posting them REGULARLY to maintain the perception that you are a "working act." Many do-it-yourself website design and hosting sites now have "blog" capabilities included in your package. There are also very inexpensive software programs that will allow you to start a blog. Type in the phrase: "Start a blog" into Yahoo, Google, or any other search engine. It can (and should) cost you very little to start a blog, so don't spend a lot of money.

11.) CREATING YOUR FINISHED ALBUM, MP3s, AND RINGTONES

Now that you have a website for your band or Solo Act, let's get you an eye-catching album cover, and let's manufacture the CD to sell! If you want to use a piece of artwork instead of a photo, get a visual artist who needs the exposure to do it for you for free (or better yet, pay them any amount that you can afford for a "one shot deal"). As far as a photograph of you or your Act, get a photographer from a school (or from www.craigslist.com; again, be careful when you're screening them). Even a simple digital photo can be uploaded into any inexpensive photo editing software (or of course, into Photoshop), where you can layer it with other photos and add eye-catching text. Try to save as much money as possible with the cover, but make sure it's very sharp.

While most people aren't foolish enough to buy a CD simply because they like the album cover, it's not an excuse to have a shabby one either. Even in the book publishing industry, the books with the fancy covers are the ones that sell more. It might be sad or even unfair, but it is true. Make your album cover a show-stopper. I am not saying it should be gaudy. There is definitely such a thing as "overkill" that can actually leave the opposite impression you hoped for. Choose carefully, and look at a lot of other album covers. You work too hard on your music to present it in a brown paper bag, or to blow off getting a cool cover for it.

Now we have your CD and the artwork for your album cover. The next step is to manufacture the physical product. But first, we need to get you a barcode for your CD before we head to a manufacturer. This way, SoundScan can count your sales in online and retail sales, and you can put yourself "on the map" when you sell. SoundScan is the official sales counter for the music industry. You want to get credit for EVERY sale you make (including all live shows at venues that work with SoundScan). To get credit for albums that you sell at shows, be sure to sign up for SoundScan's Venue Verification.

If you have the music completed on CD, ready to be duplicated, have chosen a title for the record, and you also have your artwork (or, even if you don't have your artwork, but the album is finished, AND READY to be pressed), go to www.cdbaby.com and sign your album up for independent distribution. What's wonderful about CD Baby is that they will issue you a barcode for a very small fee, and you can download it and save it to your computer instantly when you sign your album up for independent distribution. Once you have signed up your new album (again, do not worry if it has not been pressed, or if you don't have artwork; just make sure the actual album is ready), they will ask you to send them 5 compact discs for their warehouse. Go get the CD's manufactured immediately, and include the barcode on a CD-ROM for the manufacturers to include on the back of your album. Go with a large, reputable CD Manufacturer like www.discmakers.com or www.oasiscd.com (or any other well-established company). In terms of ordering smaller amounts of CD units (which I think makes sense at least initially when you're starting out at sales), a company like www.shortstacks.com is great for ordering smaller amounts of finished, packaged albums (with your barcode) on CD.

Now, let's get to the artwork, if you haven't already…

If you choose not to save your money by creating your own artwork or having someone do it for you "on the cheap," you can always throw money at the problem. A company like Discmakers, or any other large CD manufacturer that has been around for a while, can make a professional-quality, professionally-designed cover and logo for you when you send them your music for duplication. Oasis will also do this for you. If you have done your own artwork, a CD manufacturer will tell you what "format" (JPEG file, Photoshop file, etc.) and what "measurements" your artwork must be in for pressing, and you can either email them the files, or send them on a CD-ROM through "snail mail." While some manufacturers will let you upload your music as MP3's, instantly for duplication, I would <u>caution</u> against doing this, as there clearly IS a loss in sound quality from an MP3, versus a WAVE file. Go ahead and "snail mail" your CD to them, or send it Priority or 24 hour if you find yourself impatient.

Make sure you type out ALL credits, songs, and album content for the inside and back sleeve(s). Write descriptions of your songs so people understand what they're listening to, and include lyrics if you choose to. You can, of course, "go all out" financially, but why bother? While many Artists start with pressing 1,000 CD's, it might behoove you to start out with about 200 CD's and make sure they sell first. It will cost you a little more per unit, but if you're on a serious budget and no one knows who you are yet, 200 CD's is more than enough, and it will still cost you less than having 1,000 made to use as furniture in your home. This above all, especially in terms of cutting down costs, there is nothing better than an album that is "lean and mean" in design, with a well-crafted visual design. You must (I repeat) you MUST display your website address on your CD and in the sleeve. You want to let consumers and fans know where they can join your mailing list, buy tickets for your shows, and (of course) purchase more of your CD's, digital downloads, and ringtones.

Go get your CD done as soon as possible. Make a choice which manufacturer you are going to use, give them a call, and get the ball rolling. Cdbaby is waiting for their five copies.

Now, let's talk about www.amazon.com. This is the world's largest online shopping network. Amazon.com is great because it gives you the opportunity to sell your CD along with other major label and well-established acts. Selling your music on Amazon.com can only spell "name value" for you. Most importantly, you have (hopefully) already gotten the barcode for your CD from CD Baby.com, as having a barcode is a requirement if you want to be included on Amazon.com. Amazon also has its "Talent Acquisition Program," which allows you to expose your CD to various companies who are looking for your style of music. The Talent Acquisition Program is also available to Artists who create books and other creative materials. When you sign up as a seller on Amazon, you have a "control panel" of features to handle your accounting and the supply of CD's you send to their warehouse(s). You will also find many options for marketing your CD or other products on the Amazon website. You would need to get a barcode for all your products if you wanted them to be included on the site.

The Uniform Code Council is the official "issuer" of barcodes to U.S. companies, that starts with a fee for multiple products. However, you really don't need to seek out the Uniform Code Council just yet, unless you want to spend all that extra money. For your music CD, you are going to get your barcode through CD Baby. However, let's say you have a book, DVD, or any other product OF YOUR OWN that you want to sell on Amazon.com, or get into retail stores on your own. There is no need to seek out The Uniform Code Council for only a few "ala carte" products. You can purchase barcodes, one at a time, from a company like:

www.buyabarcode.com, as well as MANY others. Just type in the word "barcode" into any search engine. Using a company like this might be a much better option than spending the extra money going to The Uniform Code Council. Just use your own discretion. In regard to writing and marketing your own books, a company like: www.lulu.com is the greatest print-on-demand "suite" imaginable. Lulu can get your books onto Amazon for you, and publishing the actual book through Lulu is free. Lulu can also provide you with a barcode and distribution of your book titles (and other media titles) through Amazon.com and Barnes & Noble's online store (as well as other retail and distribution outlets).

Now, once you've gotten your CD into Cd Baby and Amazon, you'll want to make sure it is available to as many Independent online retailers as possible. This will require some research on your part. On the topic of CD Baby, please know that you are given your own webpage for your music, where you insert your bio and photo(s) along with the 2 minute sound samples and all your albums that are available for purchase through their website.
CD Baby will actually upload the 2 minutes sampled songs that you designate for them once they receive your music. Your CD Baby webpage should NOT (I repeat) should NOT be used in place of getting your OWN website! You will LINK your CD Baby page to your regular band website, and not use it as a substitute for having a website of your own. Make sure you develop and build your CD Baby (and Amazon) webpages, even though you also have your own website.

12.) HOW TO EASILY GET DIGITAL DISTRIBUTION FOR YOUR MUSIC

Apple itunes sells the majority of music downloads on the planet. They offer you MAJOR name value, prestige, and a decent cut for your digital sales. There are tons of other companies (MSN, AOL, just to name a couple) who also offer digital downloads. There are dozens and dozens of larger and smaller download companies that do this for you, and the portion of payment(s) you receive from each song will vary by the company.

CD Baby is going to be your golden gateway to the world of digital distribution for your music CD. Let them handle everything. It is easier to make your songs available for download through CD Baby than from any other sources, especially at this stage of your career. Please also keep in mind that, even if a person "listens" to your song but doesn't actually purchase the song as an MP3, you will still be paid for a "paid listen."

You are going to send CD Baby your five copies of your brand new, finished album, packaged, designed, shrink wrapped, WITH your barcode on the back of the CD. Once CD Baby has received your CD and uploaded your sample tracks/made the album "officially" in-stock and available for sale, you will log into your account and "opt-in" to the various digital distribution options that are tirelessly arranged and worked out for your advantage. Once you have opted in, it will take several weeks for your songs to be either "accepted" or "rejected" by the individual digital companies, and then "ingested" into their systems for sale. This is why it is so important for your recordings to be of high quality. You will most likely be accepted by most of them, but there are no guarantees. Your accounting and payments will be handled/sent to you through CD Baby, and all of your accounting information for both CD and

digital sales is available online within your account at any time. Be thankful for this. CD Baby will send you checks in increments as low as $10.00, $20.00, or much larger amounts, as you prefer. You can specify what amounts you would like to be paid in by logging into your account. Another company that specializes in CD release and digital distribution/online accounting is: www.tunecore.com, which (happens to) boast some celebrities who use their services. CD baby has been around "longer."

You should definitely create ringtones of your songs, since they are so easy to create and cost NOTHING to make and have available to the public. Many companies exist online that you can upload your MP3 files to for creating ringtones that you (yourself) can edit and make available for sale through the ringtone company's website, while utilizing THEIR online ringtone editing software (free of charge). One such company is: www.myxer.com, which allows you to create your own ringtones AND wallpaper (if you would like to market wallpaper of your Act, website, or "brand."

13.) HOW TO GET YOUR ONLINE SALES VEHICLE UP AND RUNNING

You will want to "link" your sales page for your CD's and digital downloads to your website and, more importantly, choose Apple itunes as your primary download format, selling both your downloads and your CD's directly from your own music website. Linking to a remote sales page or streaming audio page from your own music website may decrease clicks on the music and, ultimately, SALES. Please also keep in mind that setting up separate links to your Apple itunes page, MSN page, AOL page, and other big name pages is a very smart idea. You might want to even make the decision to feature your Apple itunes store as your

preferred seller of your downloads, since so many people who regularly buy music mp3s have the itunes software already installed on their desktops, which is necessary to complete the purchase in the first place. The largest majority of your sales will (likely) come from sales on Apple itunes. They are the biggest and most well-known, and this is definitely a case where it is truly wiser to go with "the big guys." It is a very prestigious opportunity indeed and, again, one to be thankful for.

Digital sales are the true direction that all media are heading towards (in so many respects), and you will already be available within the "Top Tier" of distributors. Make sure your album is READY. The most important pre-requisite is that your music is contained on a packaged album or EP with a barcode. If your music is bypassed for ingestion, the reason would probably be due to the quality of sound in the recording, rather than criticisms of the song itself. Please keep production quality close in mind. Make sure the recording is of very high quality.

14.) MYSPACE MUSIC (& Social Media Mayhem)

The music world has already given overwhelming importance to www.myspace.com, and having a myspacemusic page. This means that you should build a myspace page for your music (in the myspacemusic section). Please keep in mind that the reason for having such a page is to promote album sales, digital downloads, and of course, your live shows (which we will talk about more in a moment). Do NOT forget about www.facebookcom, www.twitter.com, and many of the other newer (but hugely successful) social networking websites out there.

The feature in myspace that allows you to "blast out" invites to your "friends" list is highly convenient. You are going to link your

myspace page to your main music website, and link your main music website to your myspace page as well as other social media websites. You will want to familiarize yourself with all of their consoles, and learn how to properly grow your "friends" and/or "networking list," based on your specific music genre. While myspace is generally used by regular folks for the purposes of social networking (and even dating), your purpose in the myspacemusic section (which is what you will sign up for instead of the regular section), is to PROMOTE YOUR MUSIC FOR SALES. Please beware of companies that offer illegal "robots" that flood your page with untargeted friends/fans, and send out unsolicited emails that can get your site "flagged" by the myspace team, thus subjecting your account to possible deletion. With this said, there are legitimate marketing companies that will custom-build your myspace page for you, as well as promote your music and shows to targeted members (for a fee). Be very careful here, and make sure you are working with a company that does not operate in violation of any myspace rules (as many and most of the companies that offer cheap "robot" software are in violation of the rules, and can get you canned).

This above all, make sure your myspacemusic page is clean, lean, and not flooded with so many fancy graphics that it takes forever and a day to load. What is equally important is making sure that, in the "comments" area of your page (where members can post pictures, ads, and thoughts for all to see), you do not allow people to place "mile long" and highly obnoxious banners, advertisements, and other things that "pollute" your page, slow down page loading time, and above all, "use you" by taking up more than their fair share of space endorsing something that you do not necessarily approve of. Also (and what might be worse), you want to make sure that no one is posting unauthorized or inappropriate comments about you or anyone else on your page, especially without your knowing it. There is an <u>easy</u> way to avoid any of the concerns noted above. Make sure that you <u>lock</u> (I repeat) <u>lock</u> your comments page in the settings of your myspace console (and all other social media formats). This will prevent any comments or pictures from showing up on your page unless you login and approve them first. The other party can still place the comments or banner(s), but they will have to be "approved" by you before they appear for all to see. You will receive an automatic email indicating that a comment and/or photo is there for you to "approve" or "disapprove."

Here is an example of a company that builds and promotes myspace pages for clients that pay. The website address is: <u>www.mysocialmarketing.com</u>. Also, you must go to <u>www.addthis.com</u> (it's completely FREE). Addthis.com is one of the most important websites you need to visit as soon as you have completed your own music website. You will install on your own music website, FREE of charge, a "Share" button from the html code you can easily copy and paste into the html code on your own site. If you have seen these buttons before, they are on all the MAJOR blogs and websites that are dominating the industry and the search engines. Professional universities also have these "Share" buttons on their web pages. The button is a new and cutting-edge addition to your site, and it is VERY convenient for visitors to share your site and promote it on major social marketing networks (and the like). Immediately following this passage is a list of all social marketing networks (and email options) that this (single) button can effortlessly link your site with for others to

come to your site and link with their social networks and/or websites:

1.) *Email*
2.) *Print*
3.) Digg
4.) MySpace
5.) Google
6.) Twitter
7.) *Favorites*
8.) Delicious
9.) Facebook
10.) Windows Live
11.) StumbleUpon
12.) Fifty-five more online places, including a link that can add your music to someone's "wishlist" on Amazon.com.

15.) A WORD ABOUT RECORD POOLS

For those of you who are unfamiliar with what a Record Pool is, let me explain; Record pools are services that collect music from Artists, bands, and record labels for the purpose of distributing it to deejays who need it. Many deejays subscribe to a Record Pool in order to cost-effectively get their hands on the newest music as well as add to their catalogs. Obviously, there is the potential to get serious exposure for your music, especially when you consider that certain deejays and other professionals who subscribe to the pool might also have some contacts that could be beneficial to you. Traditionally, Record Pools require the Artist or label to supply them with music in the form of records or CDs (but usually records). However, with the lucky advent of digital music distribution, many Record Pools (claim) to offer Artists and labels the ability of getting their music to a multitude of deejays via the

use of digital delivery systems. Exposure like this only has the potential to do good things, which is why I encourage you to research various Record Pools to contribute your music towards (especially if it is good for spinning at clubs).

Record Pools are organizations run by circuits of deejays that give Artists the opportunity to contribute a set number of vinyl records (or perhaps compact discs) to be spun at clubs and industry events. It costs money to supply a record pool with records, and the cost might not justify the means, unless of course you have a smashing hit song, you are performing live, and an influential deejay takes notice of the value of your music. Joining a record pool is not something that will necessarily equate with sales but, if you are an Artist looking for exposure in Clubs (and particularly, if you are a dance or electronic/R&B/Hip-hop Artist, it may be a fantastic way to network if you can continuously supply them). Not unlike the prospect of getting a prospective employer's attention through polite follow-up and visits to the Clubs, what you really need to do is PLAY there.

Here is an example of a database of record pools: www.recordpools.com. There are many other databases across the country. Also, here is an example of a company that manufactures vinyl records for distribution to Clubs. There are many websites to go to, but the one I mention as an example is: www.vinyl-record-pressing.com, since they offer discount pricing.

16.) YOUR MUSIC VIDEO (OR LACK THEREOF)

You NEED a music video. You DON'T NEED a music video. You NEED a music video. You DON'T NEED a music video. Do you understand the point here? It does not matter either way whether you have a music video. If having a music video does not

help, then it certainly will not hurt you either (unless of course the video is simply awful). The truth is, I love music videos, and it might help your career and your sense of musical presence (you could use a little extra "on-screen narcissism" to get you started) if you get a music video done. I am going to explain how you should go about this, and we are going to follow the KISS method.

First of all, we are in a whole new world of video production, and it IS a far easier and less expensive world we are living in WHEN IT COMES TIME FOR FINDING CLEVER WAYS TO SHOOT A MUSIC VIDEO INEXPENSIVELY (if you know where to go, and what to do). Like it or not, we are in the age of "digital video" which is often used to make "digital, full-length films," AS WELL AS three and a half minute music videos.

In addition, many film schools are offering students courses for shooting their films using digital cameras rather than traditional cameras that require developing. It is really much cheaper to make a digital music video, but I am not going to sit here and tell you that many "so-called Connoisseurs" will not turn their noses up over digital film, in favor of old-school cellulose. There is often a difference in the texture of the picture, but digital video is very clean and crisp (with the sound quality exemplary). Also, many and most digital films that are promoted and/or entered into festivals, etc. are converted to regular film anyway for screen viewing. However, your movie screen (at least right now) is not a movie screen, but a television screen or computer screen; and not unlike the earlier topic I mentioned about the average music listener not knowing the difference between a digital audio recording, an analog audio recording, or even an audio recording that has either been "mastered" or "not mastered," the average teenaged music fan and the adult person (alike) are not going to take notice of whether or not your music video was shot in digital

or regular film, nor are they going to care, as long as it is WELL-DONE, WELL-EDITED, and most importantly, the song and performance YOU chose for the music video was an EXCELLENT CHOICE.

Perhaps you enjoy www.youtube.com. Youtube is a company with a "universe-sized" database of film, TV, music videos, and home videos uploaded by "regular folks" and "professional film makers" alike for your viewing pleasure (or displeasure), and for the benefit of "exposure" for the person who uploaded the video. Youtube is really a fascinating invention. My mentioning of Youtube is to illustrate that, if digital cameras and "laptop computer editing" were not being used about a thousand times more frequently than regular film, Youtube might not exist, because professional and semi-professional filmmakers (and regular, suburban home video makers) would not be able to upload their videos to Youtube, and Youtube would not even exist if films could not be shot digitally. We all know that digital home video cameras have been around for a quite a period of time, but now there are cameras that can create a "broadcast-quality" music video for far less money and time. The secret is often in the "editing" of the video. Unlike the all-expensive "Avid editing system" (which is of course preferred, and which is to the film editor what Protools is to the professional recording engineer, a substantial portion of computers and laptops for sale at regular, discount electronic and office supply stores have a video editing suite capable of doing a professional job (if it has the SKILL of a professional working the mouse), despite the fact that it is not Avid. Recall what I said earlier about laptop recording software or even the 4-track analog recording process combined with the use of Nero Wave Editor and Nero Burning Rom; once the music video is "completed" (and EDITED), and/or once your song is "completed," NO ONE is going to know the process by which you

created your masterpiece, the average consumer is not going to care, and above all, it is none of anybody's business how you craft your productions (and this includes the industry, unless of course you trust the person as an "ally of yours"). The Industry likes Artists who can save them money by creating their OWN productions, and in this day and age, you really don't have a choice.

The following is an example of a website address to a company that offers music video promotion and music video "pools." The company is called: Rock America Music, and their website address is: www.rockamericamusic.com. Typing in the phrase "music video promotion" (or something similar) into the Yahoo or Google search engine(s) would not hurt, especially if you were focusing on promoting your music video to "one source a day." There are music video production company databases within many of the reference websites offered in this book, but you might want to go to www.craigslist.org and place an ad under the film and TV section in your local city, "broadcasting" the fact you need a music video and are looking for someone who needs the exposure, but is willing to work for smaller pay. Again, the secret is in the editing, which should be "quick" and in rhythm with your song. A bad editing job is a bad editing job, even if it was done using Avid. A good editing job is a good editing job, even if you used a "home" version of editing software. It comes down to the person editing the video, and not all editors are created "equally." It ALSO comes down to your performance, so don't BLAME the Editor if your performance is terrible. Make sure you REHEARSE!

Try to save some money when shooting your video, but take the time with your "look" and the "scenery." Get a storyline going, if at all possible. You don't want to do a music video with a quick "styling" that looks as though it was "thrown together in a hurry."

Try typing the phrase: "how to direct your own music video" (or something similar, including: "music video production companies") into yahoo or google, and see what pops up. Make sure your music video is very well-done (even if it is done "on the cheap"), and try to shoot it in high definition digital video (if you choose digital video over film).

My ultimate vision for your music video is that it is front and center when people visit your music website, that it is also on your myspace.com music website, and that it is on Youtube as well. Then, you need to promote its likeness to venues and businesses that broadcast music videos (or something similar). Clothing stores and novelty gift stores that play music videos in their shops are a great place to offer your music video for customers to "view" and "hear" while they shop, along with postcards to your website address or free music samples. There are companies that specialize in providing music video content to retail businesses as well (but you might not have or want to spend the money). Just follow the (minimum of) "one a day" rule. The better your music video comes out, the more inspired you will be to push it. If the video does not put your "best foot forward," do not "push it" just because you have "completed it." Do something different, like another music video that DOES put your "best foot forward." If you are promoting your music CD and having success, you can certainly put together a DVD of music video(s) and/or your live concert footage for sale as a compilation, and most of the companies that can handle your music CD manufacturing will also handle DVD manufacturing.

17.) YOUR RADIO PLAY (OR LACK THEREOF)

A lot of Artists and bands spend a ton of money paying for radio promotion and airplay through various companies that offer

this service to Independent Artists and bands. I am not mentioning any of them in this book. It is not that many are not legitimate (although many ARE NOT legitimate). As a new Act, you will not have a shot at major airplay at a major radio station if you do not have sales. Your sales are the most important. Many people boast airplay at radio stations, but the problem is that they are telling you about this when you are asking them "how their music career is going" as they are ringing up the DVD you are renting at the cash register of the video store where they work. Do not worry about radio play for now. Just worry about sales. When you have enough sales of music, you have bartering power when seeking to obtain a record deal. Nothing else will matter. If you are fixed on getting radio play and wish to hire a radio promotion company, prepare to pay thousands of dollars for very little difference in your life. The choice is yours to make.

18.) DO-IT-YOURSELF PRECAUTIONS

I am a firm believer in the importance of being a "do-it-'yourselfer,'" and taking care of anything and everything you can on your own, whenever possible. I believe in the importance of having a brick-and-mortar work ethic, and have always had a brick-and-mortar work ethic myself. Yet, I have also learned through my own experiences that there is a legitimate danger in going overboard with this philosophy. If you are the only "brains or ambition" in your band, and you regularly take the extra initiative to read books like this without any urging from others, or if you are a Solo Artist or Songwriter following the same strict code of sacred, faith-produced self-discipline, it is often so easy to become "so busy" wearing "so many different hats" (Artist, Writer, Producer, Performer, Web Designer, Promoter, Manager, Booking Agent, Retailer, etc.) that it becomes a vicious yet "addictive" cycle that one might have difficulty letting go of. We

all need to remind ourselves that we cannot, and many times, SHOULD NOT be doing everything for ourselves. Be willing to accept help from others. That is the only way that you will "grow."

The most important thing to keep in mind is that you are the TALENT! You are (often) the one that every other person involved in the production (or not involved in the production) WISHES that they could be, but cannot. You should be focusing on writing, recording, and performing music. Therefore, it is not a crime to allow others to handle (various) web, myspace, online promotion updates, etc. while you focus on being the Artist. Being wise enough to create a balance which enables you to politely "delegate tasks to willing people" does NOT make you a lazy person.

While keeping everything mentioned above in mind, it is also important to understand that so much of the "scum" and "the growth" that floats along the surface of this often cruel business still tries to pass itself off as "part of the industry." Many of these folks are in a constant tug-of-war for your hard-earned money. Any Promoters, Labels, or "so-called Managers" that require ANY fees whatsoever (even $2.00 for a listening fee; *pathetic*) are people you run away from and (not) walk away from. Above all, this is NOT what I mean when I tell you to get other people to help you. There are more scammers in this business than there are "legitimate people." You need to learn the difference and know the difference, as this is a very dirty business, indeed.

Sometimes, it is okay to spend money on things that will save you precious time if you choose to. You can refer to this as the option of "throwing money at the problem instead." The types of things that one can throw money at are things like design, image enhancement (if you are really clueless and fashionably challenged), web updates, and other costly ventures (time wise,

that is), like taking a trip to an Art School, spending money and time making advertising posters for bulletin boards at the Student Center, just to find a student photographer or graphic designer etc., and then ending up with work that does not make the cut, working with an unreliable or over-inundated student, or perhaps just having the spare time and hours to do your own work on an album cover. It is nice to know you have these other talents, but what is more important to you, music or graphic design work? You can throw money at the problem only if you have the money to spend, and you know that spending it will save you time and not cause problems for you down the road.

The thing to remind yourself, once again, about being a "loyal do-it-yourselfer" is that, if you get too locked into it, the old habits will die hard. A truly successful Act has an Agent, Manager, Lawyer, Publicist, Stylist, Web Designer, Manufacturer, Distributor, and on and on and on. The divine beauty and spirit that is embedded within your genuine talent can be found in your ability to (inevitably) do all these things yourself in the beginning. Just remember that the most important thing left out here, yet which suffers "the most" from neglect (as you switch from hat to hat to hat) is your music. This is why it is important to find creative ways of inspiring others to help as you implement ways of delegating jobs to others.

19.) YOUR LIVE SHOW

You want to be playing out at clubs a minimum of twice a month or, ideally, once a week. You will create a calendar section on your website and list your shows in advance, as well as sell tickets online and at the venue. www.ifanz.com (which is owned by Paul McCartney) has everything you need to start doing all this, and a basic membership is free. Again, you must be playing live,

unless you are a songwriter pitching your songs, if you want to be successful as an Act. If you are not performing, you are still obligated (to yourself) to get your finished music (product) out there, even if you're (literally) *only* following the "do one thing a day" rule.

The simplest way to start forming relationships at clubs that you would like to play at is to go to the club during business hours, find the booking agent, and POLITELY introduce yourself with your CD, a WONDERFUL photo, press (if you have any), and a biography that is interesting, but not filled with any "fluff." Have an interesting story ready "yourself" that is "human." Do not sell short the concept of doing some open mic nights at clubs. This is a very easy way to let the hosts know who you are, and that you are willing to start from the bottom and work your way up to get a gig there. Often times, you will only have to play one open mic night to prove to them that you can perform. There are many clubs that offer the (simple) requirement that you play an open mic night, stand in the "dreaded" line of musicians to sign up on the roster sheet (just once), only to get a gig afterwards if you speak with them, especially AFTER your performance. There are also websites on the Internet that offer databases of clubs that have open mic nights. The Songwriter's Guild of America (www.songwritersguild.com) has a database of all open mic nights in the state of California, yet they are building a database to include all 50 states. Get your favorite song from your repertoire "polished and ready," call a club to find out which evening they have their open mic night, and get out there! Remember, this is the best way to book your own gig(s).

There is also a company called www.onlinegigs.com that offers musicians the opportunity to connect with venues for gigs. The Sonic bids Corporation: www.sonicbids.com is also listing venues

and allowing Artists to submit their Electronic Press Kits (EPKs) to venues in their database. You should probably join sonic bids and get an electronic press kit to send to clubs, industry, and media. Also, if you join a local chapter of the American Federation of

Musicians, they can help you get gigs as well. Ideally, the "personal touch" is best by going out and introducing yourself to booking agents POLITELY and non-intrusively, presenting yourself "polished" and "professionally," and doing an open mic night at clubs that require it as a form of "initiation." When you do develop your live show, make sure you are making full use of the stage, and that you are doing something unique that makes you stand out from the rest of the Acts. You have all the imagination in the world to accomplish this task because you are an Artist. You do not even need to be told "not to be like everybody else," but I am saying it anyway because competition is fierce. Do something different. Make the audience think that your performance is rare and special (because it is)!

20.) PROMOTING YOUR LIVE SHOW

Promoting your Live Show is NOT easy work, but it is something that must be done if you want to build a team of fans who will come out to support you. You will have to pound the pavement. If you can get a pile of people towards the front of the stage, then the show is not a waste (especially if you can sell a pile of CD's). Do not be discouraged if you get a small turn-out when you are just starting out. There is always that "one" club date where the place is empty and you want to quit. Keep going. The key thing to understand is that, if you network with other working bands, you can plan to headline or be included in their roster, which will expose your music to many of their fans and, perhaps, turn them into your own, too. Also, www.myspace.com now has "street team" services to promote your music, and so do a

multitude of other companies. While no one will make a better promoter than yourself, the reality is that you cannot do it alone.

Have CD Samplers made, hand them out, describe what your music is about to people (at coffee shops, bars, and where young people congregate), and if you cannot stand the idea of hitting the streets, then hire someone to help you, or have your friends help you. Get posters and samplers displayed at shops that sell clothing and items (that might be geared to your music or message), and target (at least) one business each day. Tell them you would like to do a show for the customers in their store, then promote your CD and venue dates for future shows. Get everybody's email address and keep them constantly updated on your music, constantly leaving the impression that you are a working Act. The most important thing you should know is that selling music CD's and digital downloads is the only thing that matters. Make sure you sell CDs at your show, and sign up with SoundScan Venue Verification to get credit for your sales. "If you sell the most chocolates, you will win the top prize," that is, Industry will want to know what you are doing. After all, you will have proven that you can sell.

21.) ALL HAIL THY HOLY PUBLICIST

All right! You have got your CD with a barcode, you have a website that can sell your CD, you are being placed in Apple I-tunes and in all the other digital download content providers, you have photography, and you even have some gigs. Let us start here with a very important word of caution, and then let's catapult all your impressive hard work (with the above) into the air for all to witness *and* hear.

In a business that is surrounded with scammers and con-artists who will promise you the moon and the stars in all music areas, ranging from radio promotion to deal shopping to press, there are also a whole other breed of "consultants" who will tell you that you should never pay a dime to anyone to do anything for you that you can do for yourself. They will tell you to handle everything yourself, and give you the "false" feeling of complete power and control over your career (where yes, you do have complete power and control over your career and, no, you should not be handling or even speaking with industry/media yourself to secure an interview, etc. if you can successfully avoid having to). It looks unprofessional. You can develop your own relationships with music media and other media through personal letters, including story slants aimed towards various subjects in media that will write a review of your music because of its cultural relevance to their readers (and not necessarily *because* it's music), but this should only be a supplemental effort. <u>You need someone to represent you.</u> It is much more professional. Unsolicited, as unfortunate as this sounds, often means unimportant, which I am sure you have had to endure in the past. A manager is one thing, but a good publicist can be equally valuable, if not MORE so. It is unprofessional much of the time to walk around with the delusion that industry people will regard you as "important" just because you think that you are (and the worst part about this is that you ARE). Again, the most important thing to remember about being a "do-it-'yourselfer'" is that, when reality kicks in, you cannot do everything yourself, ESPECIALLY if you are solo! There is no reason to reinvent the wheel. You should have as many people helping you as possible. The consultant who tells you to be your own manager, publicist, promoter, marketer, and advertiser (likely) wants you to give your money over and over again to HIM/HER instead, and *not* the Publicist. In the meantime, your work is going

nowhere, although you are certainly getting a lot of knowledge you cannot possibly implement all by yourself. After all, how many hats can one possibly wear before losing the mind inside one's head? Before I continue, let me mention the all-important distinction that a Publicist is someone you DO pay, and a Manager is someone you NEVER pay.

The idea that you can do all your own PR and promotions without having to pay for anything is unrealistic. Yes, you "can" do it. But you will likely not get the largest results possible. You are a Musician and Artist. You should be writing music and songs, and you should be performing (and taking care of yourself). Time is too valuable and short. Let a specialist handle working with the all-important press. They will often get you on a TV show or in a magazine that is otherwise out of your reach (unless you want to spend time doing a year of follow-up for a "maybe" followed by a rejection).

Again, the motive often involved with many "consultants" for independent artists is that they would rather have you give thousands of dollars to *them* instead of to a publicist. In some ways, a good consultant can serve like a very expensive, but very GOOD book, and just as one should handle all valuable books with dignity, one should also neatly and respectfully release the book in excellent shape so that somebody else may "read" and "learn." You'll also save extra money down the road, since consultants are so expensive and only valuable for a period of time. The WORK is your responsibility. This is the most polite way of handling any consultant who has done all for you that they will (ever) be capable of doing. Yet, the publicist (if he/she is a good publicist) has carefully cultivated working relationships with magazines, newspapers, television shows, even music companies/promoters, over a period of many years and, again (if he/she is a good publicist), these various media companies begin to rely on him/her for something juicy because they "trust" that the Publicist will deliver the goods. Many publicists can also get press to come to your live shows. If a consultant tells you not to pay a publicist and to do your own publicity, just walk into the mailroom of an average newspaper and look at the bags and bags filled with press releases that never reach the light of day because a small handful that are not in those bags are being personally pitched by a publicist who should, in fact, be representing *your* story.

Now, the most important thing for you to know is that you should be very careful when choosing a Publicist because the world of scammers attempts to populate the world of Publicists as well, and often succeeds. Publicists are very expensive. Try to go with the best, though. I will give you a strategy in a moment if you cannot afford one. Start with: www.prfirmfinder.com, which is a national database. Again, just because it is listed, does not mean it is the best. This is true on any website, or in any advertisement. Do they specialize in music, or do they also handle books and other media? If you are a multi-faceted Artist, you should go with a Publicity Firm who handles things within your realm so you can switch to different artistic mediums over the years while you develop and grow your relationship with the publicist (and of course your career).

Examine the companies' clients and connections very carefully, and check to see if there is a file on the company at the Better Business Bureau (www.bbb.org). Also, check to see how long they have been in business. Regarding a publicity firm's media contacts and clients, if they are legitimate, they will BOAST these things. Also, make sure you develop a good rapport with them. Some publicists are very good, but if you do not "vibe" with them, get out as fast as you can, and do not give them a dime. If your gut tells you not to trust them, LISTEN to your gut, despite what they might promise you, and get out as fast as you can. There are thousands of publicity firms and publicists dying to promote you for a price. Find someone better. The ideal situation is to have a close, working relationship with a publicist based in the SAME city as you (or a close, "nearby city") so that you can meet in-person, bring the most out of them, and vice-versa. Creative publicists who can think of different story and marketing angles will work better for you, and so will a publicist who can help train you for media appearances (some DO), so that you appear "top notch." Publicists are just people, so go with a person you "like," but who also has the media contacts you NEED.

Here is an idea if you are scrapped for money. Some will tell you to approach a car dealership or a clothing company and tell them you'll do shows at their place of business or advertise their logo and/or services, etc. on your marketing materials for your act in exchange for sponsorship money. Do you really think they will be that excited? These might be decent things to do, but here is a different slant. Whatever your music happens to be about, you had better align yourself with a cause or charity, if not tangibly, then also within the messages of your lyrics, catering to various groups of people in need. Any business has the potential to give you sponsorship money, but most Artists do not know exactly what to do with the money (if) they get it. Your goal of attaining sponsorship money for your act from a business is to use the money for a Publicist with serious connections. An automobile dealership or bank would love to hear of the attention you will get them during your all-important TV, radio, or magazine/newspaper interview, and how it would not be possible for you to spread the word about your music, your cause, and how the cause is written about in your music if it was not for the generous support of a particular company, and how much they care for needy children, breast cancer research, or any other cause that reaches your heart. Interviews secured through a Publicist with a thank you during the interview from you to your sponsor equals advertising ALONG with a positive, socially conscious presentation for the company AND for you. By giving you money, they will be getting advertising. Be sure to suggest this to them as tactfully as you can. Bring your media kit and your message with you. Make your music second in importance to your philanthropic mission. The goal is to get sponsorship money for a publicist with the connections you need. Make sure your website is up and running and that you have CD's for sale online so that when people visit your site, they can buy CD's and learn about your next show and/or public event, which should also be listed.

22.) REALISTIC NUTRITIONAL GOALS (and the low-sodium V-8 reality).

I am not going to lecture you on eating right, but some of you probably have horrible eating habits. I sympathize with you, and I am often in the same boat. It is so very difficult to eat right in a fast food culture, especially in a business with no guarantees. If you are living on a lot of bacon double cheeseburgers and fries, there is hope, and there are things you can do.

It is often unrealistic for people who have been nourished throughout their lives with processed foods, fats, and empty calories to be expected to start eating healthy, at least on a "truly consistent" and "measurable" basis. A huge portion of the population does not know how to eat right anyway. The simplest thing you can do is add 2-3 eight ounce glasses of low-sodium V-8 juice to your diet each day. Think of the word "automation" here. If you are cranky about this kind of routine, then get out a very large glass and drink at least one glass a day. This is NOT medical advice, and might not even be appropriate advice for some. It is just something that has worked for me. The regular V-8 juice has a ton of sodium, which you can do without. You also might end up feeling very thirsty. But it is rather amazing to realize the improvement in mood and productivity that comes from all the vitamins and minerals in vegetable juices. If you do not buy or eat fruits and vegetables on a regular basis, buy them in a container and drink them. It is better than the burger, the fries, and the soda alone. It is also better than "nothing," it is economical, and it is realistic, based on your present habits. Also, drink as much green tea as you can (ask your doctor if it is safe for you, and if he/she says "no," get a second opinion). According to scientific research, the polyphenols in green tea are much more powerful than those found in red wine. L-theanine, the natural chemical found in green tea leaves, produces a "calming" mood (along with alpha brain waves), and its calming effect can off-set any negative effects from the (much lower) amount of caffeine in green tea (compared to coffee).

Go to google and type in the phrase: "food pyramid." Several icons of full-color food pyramids will appear at the top. Click on the one food pyramid picture that least offends you, print it in full color, and attach it to your refrigerator with a magnet. This has worked for me, along with buying a huge pile of fresh fruits and keeping them in the fridge, eating a peach and a plum for a morning breakfast or mid-day snack, followed by a fish oil capsule (again, just something that works for me, and NOT medical advice). This kind of thinking can work if you're cramped up in an office on your computer growing your business, and need to "feed" your actual *brain tissue*, in addition to your body.

Take a multiple vitamin pill every day. I usually purchase the 30 day boxed supplies of vitamins that are wrapped in individual, hermetically-sealed plastic packets. There are many different brands, and they are convenient even though they cost a bit more. There are about six pills you take at once in a specialized Men's or Women's formula of ingredients. Only buy the ones with a vitamin E pill that has NO MORE THAN 400 IU. Check the label. Anything more than that can actually cause more harm than good, according to scientific research. I often take these packets with me when I leave my home in case I have my first meal outside my home (which is often the case). You take your vitamin(s) after your first meal, every single day, and even if you only manage to eat one meal that day (which I certainly DO NOT recommend doing). In addition, take a fish oil capsule every single day. This is CRUCIAL. The typical fish oil capsule has 1,000 milligrams of omega 3 fatty acids. Research shows that omega 3 fatty acids "slick" and "lubricate" your arteries, possibly preventing heart attacks and strokes. Fish oil in higher doses can decrease depression in some people, also according to scientific research. Just start out by taking a single 1,000 milligram pill. If you want to take more, ask a doctor first. 1,000 milligrams is really all you need. Fish oil capsules are the ULTIMATE health insurance policy. You can also buy them with an enteric coating if you have a sensitive stomach. There are also flaxseed oil capsules available, which are vegetarian and contain the same amount of omega 3's. Again, ask a doctor about how many fish oil or flaxseed oil capsules you should take.

23.) COMPLETE FINANCIAL EMPOWERMENT FOR MUSICIANS

Here is a subject you might feel is something you are (somehow) not "entitled" to pay much attention to, given your choice of pursuing an often volatile entertainment career path that harbors a lot of ups and downs. You might hold the idea that many people in your life are (or have been) putting you into the category of a "struggling musician." The reality is that, if you use this term within your life at all, the chances are likely that you alone are using it, and no one else is even making such a distinction. You might even believe it is "expected" of you to be living hand to mouth and therefore, you create a self-fulfilling prophecy and actually "maintain it" because you believe you do not have a choice, and that it will not always be this way once you get your "big break." You might be right, and you should be right. But guess what? This is a business and, since you have probably (already) been told just about everywhere that you are supposed to be thinking like a businessperson, you really ought to be paying attention to money and retirement savings and areas within this category that go "beyond" your performance and/or writing career. The goal here is that you achieve "the big time" financially, even when you are experiencing "the down time." Disregard the notion of what people think or speculate about your lifestyle or career. You have an amazing gift, and you should be hearing this a lot. Here is a way you can still have all the things you want, and let the world know you are the consummate Entrepreneur (in addition to a highly creative performer and all-around genius). These ideas might sound simple, and I am praying that they not only do, but that you will also implement these (simple) ideas as well into your life. This all starts with paying yourself <u>first.</u>

Money cannot buy you happiness, but it can buy you freedom and some inner peace. The outer borders of freedom and inner peace are (virtually) without any borders at all. If you do not believe me, just ask a travel agent.

Your emotions and personal relationships are a separate matter, and should be viewed and *handled* as such if you ever hope to amass any money, but are currently preoccupied with the dauntingly dreary task(s) of paying off large loans or credit cards. Opening a savings account is great for your self-esteem AND your survival. It has the potential, in less time than one thinks, to blossom into "peace of mind" for you. The truth is that you should already have a savings account by now, if for nothing else, then for a minimum of 3-6 months of emergency living expenses. But why stop there? If you already have a savings account (again, you should), here is some insight on the best way to grow a savings account, and what it should be used for as you save throughout your life. Saving throughout your life should be the all-important virtue behind the existence of your savings account. Making it effortless, or as close to effortless as possible so that you do not even miss the money, is something this section touches upon.

First, please realize you are planting a tiny little seed in order to grow a very strong and healthy tree. If you have a savings account and it is empty, look at your task as halfway finished, since you have already created a nutrient and mineral-rich environment (with a competitive interest rate) that is just waiting for the arrival of the seed. The seed comes from your labor, so do not give it away to others. Plant the seed in the ground where it belongs, so it will pay you even more for the stressful work you do, years down the road.

The goal is to create a tiny tree and grow it into a large, blooming, giving tree, standing freely and highly above the ground, and offering you "shade, protection, and freedom." It might help you to think of the classic children's story: "The Giving Tree" by Shel Silverstein (if you haven't thought of this by now already). The tree in this wonderful story is EXACTLY how we want our tree to become. We want this tree to make us happy, too (as the tree in the story makes the boy happy until the boy has grown old and gray, and even *beyond that*). This does not happen overnight though. Be *thankful* for this.

If you nurture an initial savings seed gently, it will grow without effort, automatically, and mostly without your attention. Your savings account will start out and grow up like this with your monthly care. You may find that you have grown up a bit, too.

A simple savings account with a competitive interest rate will do just fine. This is something you can set up that does not require much research or effort. In today's economy where banks rigorously compete for your business, go with the bank that has the most competitive interest rate.

The trap I used to set for myself when attempting to save is that I would try to scrounge around and build up the account too quickly, only to end up having to tap into it early, due to required expenses. The goal is to never think about tapping into your savings, at least not for quite a period of time. We will look at how long in a moment.

Here is a simple strategy that might help: Start with $100.00 per month, which is something you should be able to stick with. If you have to do less then do less, but make sure you do it. $50.00 is okay, too. $100.00 is just *better*. Citibank offers an account called the Ultimate Savings Account. ING Direct also offers the Orange Savings Account. Both accounts can be opened online, and at Citibank, you can go in-person to a local branch if you do not have a computer, or prefer not to do any banking on a computer.

As strange as this might sound, you might want to actually avoid putting any "extra" money each month into your savings account. Use this money to pay off your debts. Just add the same amount of water, fertilizer, and T.L.C. you give your savings tree each month (which is hopefully $100.00 in cash). Again, if you put too much money in, you might end up having to withdraw from the account due to unexpected expenses, debt, and *temptations*. The tree could die, and you might have to start all over again with a tiny new seed; what a horrible thought, indeed.

If you are scratching your head at this point because you earn enough income each month where you believe you can put more than that amount of money away, or you are struggling financially but believe you will be able to make the choice of cutting out unnecessary types of spending then, by all means, put the extra money away each month! The simple strategy to employ is that you must decide and commit to a *specific* dollar amount each month, and you must commit *indefinitely*.

For the relationship and commitment-fearful people out there, this will be the easiest relationship you have ever been in. You can stick to this one without any significant effort if you commit to a figure that does not mess up your daily life. Please keep in mind that, as unfortunate as this might sound to some, it might offer some relief to many: a HUGE portion of the population, given the high cost of living today, are doing WELL for themselves if they can commit to saving $100.00 per month *successfully over time*. Think about what kind of savings you will have in just five years if you contribute just $100.00 each month into an account with compounding interest.

A savings account should have a goal that moves beyond the idea of simply filling it up with money as a safety basket that you will probably end up "munching on" and "finishing up" before the big party. I suggest having a goal while pointing out that your savings account IS your future savings basket, and that giving it a goal is like water and fertilizer for the tree YOU are nurturing. If you are living "hand to mouth" and do not know how to get out of debt, make sure the goal of your savings account is NOT to pay off your debt. Handle paying the debt off separately. If you have outstanding debt on multiple credit cards, just make the highest amount of payment you can make each month to the card with the highest interest rate until that one is paid off, and then repeat this until all cards with lesser interest rates have been paid off. Pay only the minimum payment each month on cards with the lower interest rates as you pay off as much as you can on the card with the highest interest rate first.

Your savings account is *yours to keep.* Many savings accounts offer automatic, monthly withdrawals from a checking account (or other account) directly into your savings account. I recommend going each month and making the deposit to your savings tree in-person. The trip to the bank will give you time to visualize your dreams as you experience genuine self-confidence in that same moment, knowing you are going to the bank to make your deposit because you are a responsible adult who actively participates in the construction of a solid financial future, and one who makes these wise decisions because you care about yourself and your future goals.

If you are currently renting an apartment, you might want to think about using a good portion of your savings account for a future down-payment on a home or production/recording studio. Also, it is very important to keep in mind that having a large debt should NOT stop you from having a savings account! You need to pay yourself first EVERY SINGLE TIME you earn money from your physical labor.

Buying a home and/or investing in a studio is a wise investment "for the rest of us," because a house is the most valuable investment made by most people. Houses, condominiums, office buildings, recording studios, and land in general, tends to go UP in value as the years pass, NOT down.

The idea held by many that the stock market is "a rich person's game" may or may not be true, but a savings account is in your reach. You really have no excuse. Pay yourself first, remember the value of a dollar, and just how expensive it is to live. The faint light at the end of the tunnel that IS your tiny savings seed will grow into a brilliantly blinding light over time as you nurture it and grow closer to it. The light will then begin to nurture you, too.

I want to mention one final word about stocks; you need to work with a financial advisor. At the very least, you should get yourself a subscription to the Wall Street Journal's *Smart Money* magazine. Every month, the safe, tried and true, "outlives us all" caliber stocks are reviewed by the very biggest and most successful businessmen and women of all time. There are regular recommendations for stocks listed by Warren Buffet and those who run a close race to him. I would want you to work with an advisor at the very least. If you feel you can invest on your own, the only website I would recommend to get you started is www.directinvesting.com. Here, you can begin investing from the comfort of your own home, using your computer. You should only do this if you are willing to follow the written advice of experts on the website, who take the time to present you with sample
portfolios and the top stock picks they recommend for you to invest in "for the long haul." What is wonderful and unique about www.directinvesting.com is that you can literally purchase one share at a time, typically with no trading fees whatsoever. There is a nominal yearly membership fee, and it is worth it. This gives you the opportunity to start small and to grow your portfolio.

Again, you can purchase one share at a time if you prefer. You can set your account up in such a way that enables you to reinvest your dividends automatically. Do not go it alone when doing any of this. Only follow the experts.

Even more important than the topic of investing in stocks is the establishment of your retirement account. You should start a retirement account in addition to your savings account. The two will carry you nicely over time.

You should not care if you are working at a supermarket. You still have a shot to go big-time financially and you really do have a choice. Money is money. Your dream is worth even more. Substitute teaching is a great option for musicians and songwriters because the pay level is (generally) higher than minimum wage per day, plus you can get retirement points towards a pension, even if you're just working part-time. Regardless, do not ever assume that your 401k or retirement savings plan is enough. It never really is. The ideal situation to create is the start an IRA or IRA Roth on your own. You will start an IRA Roth as your most important savings basket for the future, independent of your savings account or 401k at your job. If you only earn a very small salary and do not think it is possible to start an IRA or IRA Roth, there is hope. Fidelity Investments, or www.fidelity.com, has an excellent alternative for people with low budgets. Whatever your present age, do not let it discourage you. Fidelity offers the Simple Start IRA or IRA Roth, with automatic deductions of as little as $200.00/month. Think automation here.

You will sign up for a Fidelity Freedom Fund. This enables you to choose your own retirement year (give or take a five year range), and if you invest just $200.00/month (you can invest more up until the maximum each year if you prefer), then you will still have enough to create a nice retirement for yourself, even if you can only afford the $200.00. You can literally start online or over the phone. Charles Schwab, and a large group of other investment firms offer similar products. Fidelity has a low, attractive starting figure of $200.00. Your Freedom Fund account with automatic contributions each month, done electronically through your checking account, is truly maintenance-free. You do not have to know a single thing about investing. It is an account for your entire life. It is carefully managed each month by Fidelity, and your money is invested in a large, mixed blend of mutual funds and stocks, in this country, and overseas. The portion of money they invest from your monthly contributions towards specific investments are adjusted by Fidelity automatically each year as you get closer towards your retirement date. You do not have to do anything, and you do not have to know anything. Still, a comfortable retirement is something within your reach, regardless of where your music career happens to be.

You need a retirement account, and you should start right away if you can. Talk with a financial advisor at Fidelity, or at any investment firm of your choice. You will be glad you did.

24.) MUSIC MARKETING AND NETWORKING RESOURCES, GALORE

The following website resources have been reviewed in order to assist you with making appropriate choices for marketing your music on and offline. All of these resources can be taken advantage of from your computer at home, so make sure you are tackling *at least* one task per day.

- www.tunecore.com – This digital distribution and music promotion service is very similar to that of cdbaby.com, catering (primarily) to independent artists. What makes this company impressive is that they also have a celebrity clientele of musicians and artists who also use their services.

- www.sonicbids.com - Many people believe that the "Electronic Press kit" (aka "EPK") will eventually take over the concept/usage of the traditional, time-consuming, (and expensive) "bulky paper" Press Kit. SonicBids.com is the truly innovative company responsible for the inception of the highly economical EPK, and you can create one on their site in roughly 20 minutes. This is a subscription-based service that allows you to place your whole Music Marketing package online, ready to be blasted (via email) to media contacts (complete with files of your music), in quantities of up to 25 at a time! They also have regular, exclusive offers for members, allowing you to submit to special Music Festivals and Media Companies directly through their site. Sonic bids clearly offers a lot more to the Artist than just an EPK, so this site is definitely worth checking out. Sign up for a FREE trial of the Sonic bids EPK Service and, very importantly, if you are a Music Festival or Talent Agent yourself (or if you are holding some type of musical event), you should absolutely check out SonicBids.com now to learn how you can inform the masses of Talent about your event, or receive EPK submissions DIRECTLY FROM the masses of talent that use the Sonic bids EPK daily.

- http://a2gmusic.com – This is a database containing the contact information of record labels all over the country, as well as venues and other valuable resources and services that will save you much time in your research efforts. You can get EVERYTHING in one place, and all is found easily, alphabetically, and by state. This is a clever, useful, and intriguing website for Artists, Songwriters, and Musicians.

- www.lulu.com – Based on the type of praise this company has received by highly-respected technological magazines, as well as their easy-to-use and highly sophisticated online console, lulu.com has earned its title as one of the top print-on-demand book publishing website for writers of any kind to publish their work, give it a barcode, and make it available in many of the largest online bookstores in existence. This is a must-visit if you have books you would like to publish, but don't know where to start.

- www.wordclay.com – This highly impressive, old-school, no frills, brick-and-mortar print-on-demand company has also received kudos from top technological magazines. The industrial video on the web site that explains who they are and what they can do for serious writers is worth the trip. Wordclay appears to have better distribution options than most print-on-demand companies, and is a top choice for this (needed) service for writers.

- www.cafepress.com - At this website, you can set up a COMPLETELY FREE online store for your music merchandise, carrying every type of mug, t-shirt, sweatshirt, and novelty item you can think of, proudly displaying your band photo or company logo. You simply upload your images to a template of the item, create your own store, and set your own prices. You can even sell your music there; very, very cool indeed…

- www.musicconnection.com - This is the official magazine relating to all areas of services for Musicians and Artists, current musical events, and interviews. MC is located in Southern California. However, take advantage of the online version from ANYWHERE ON THE PLANET. The majority of resources and features are geared specifically towards the Musicians and Songwriters that religiously subscribe to it. I have used this magazine personally and have made many contacts. Also, you can place FREE CLASSIFIED ADS in this magazine if you are searching for other Musicians, Artists, or Songwriters to collaborate with.

- www.cdbaby.com – In addition to being loaded beyond belief with marketing information and bulletins of people and companies seeking music, you get your own web page for your CD, and they will even sell you a barcode for your CD (all at a VERY small cost), reporting ALL sales to SoundScan for you. Cdbaby also appears to be a "golden gateway" to getting your music uploaded to all the MAJOR digital distributors (like itunes, etc.), while taking an astonishingly SMALL percentage from your electronic sales. For CD sales, they take a $4.00 cut from the price that YOU set for your CD, and they take orders and ship the product for you. Obtaining a barcode for your cd is the smartest (and also the correct) way to get credited by SoundScan for the number of units you sell. Credit for Albums you sell on your own can eventually lead to a Record Deal with a larger company if you can push those sales up on your own, first (as you build your own brand and identity). They will *also* provide a credit card swiper for your live shows so you can sell CDs and merchandise.

- www.uc-council.org - This is the official website of the Uniform Code Council. This is the council that issues barcodes. You can sign up with them as a member to receive barcodes for your music, but (keep in mind), it will be hundreds of dollars cheaper to get a single barcode for your album through CD Baby or www.buyabarcode.com. Please be sure to (also) check other resources for obtaining your own barcode, preferably with a company that can provide barcodes for many different types of products (books, DVDs, etc.). Type the phrase "buy a barcode" (or something similar) into a search engine like Yahoo or Google.

- www.amazon.com - This is considered the most well-known online store for all "general products in existence" available in the marketplace, but they are also quite well-known for their "Amazon Advantage" program. This program enables Independent Artists to sell their CDs along with major label Artists. The good side to all this is that you are in a major store with worldwide acclaim. You absolutely should and must put your CD for sale on this site. Professionally, it is a WISE move to make for the public eye. Once again, MAKE SURE YOU HAVE A BARCODE, or they will not sell your music, or any of your own products. Once your CD is for sale on Amazon, you need to make sure your own music website gives visitors easy access to the Amazon sales page. Make sure you create a link.

- www.marketingyourmusic.com - This website is packed with every type of lesson imaginable, educating you on how to have a productive music career. It was created by

CD Baby's (original) founder/owner, Derek Sivers. All necessary skills and tips are addressed, and can be learned if you do not know them already.

- www.allrecordlabels.com - This is a VERY cool site. It has over 24,000 record labels in its database, and everything is organized according to genre. Also, the site advertises many other sites and services that give you the opportunity to promote your songs. This is definitely worth checking out.

- www.ezineseek.com - As an Artist, Songwriter, or Musician, it is imperative that you build a solid online presence in addition to your offline, traditional forms of marketing your work. An ezine is basically an online, virtual magazine. Getting published or reviewed in ezines is an excellent way to build an online presence by generating publicity for you and driving people to your website. Most (if not all) ezines that feature you will create a link directly to your site. Since many of you might not know where to begin looking for ezines that are appropriate for your musical style (since the Internet is huge and literally the size of a virtual universe flooded with ezines), this particular website should help get you started. Search it creatively and wisely, and do not believe (for a moment) that ezines of a non-musical nature are worth skipping. Perhaps the subject matter in your music might be valuable to their reader's interests.

- www.topica.com - This is one of the most comprehensive and complete websites to visit for setting up and managing an email and newsletter system for your music. It is truly an online "suite." As your fan list or contact base grows, you will undoubtedly need to manage them and should be doing this from the very beginning of your career. There is a basic, 14 day (FREE) option within this site that you can take advantage of. There are also options with fancier gadgets for a fee.

- www.learningannex.com - I include this site because I have taken a business-related course here, and want to take just about every other course this amazing organization offers each month. If you do not live near the locations, you can take many of the courses conveniently online. They frequently offer many seminars geared specifically to Artists and Songwriters, and are usually taught by a numerous amount of music industry veterans. I know that Miles Copeland has taught seminars at the Learning Annex before. Please go to this site, as they cover so many subjects in all walks of life that can catapult your success in just about anything. I think The Learning Annex is truly one-of-a-kind.

- www.filmfestivals.com - Take all of the misery and headache of finding Independent and larger-scale films to pitch your music to and throw it out the window now. This website will keep you in the know of all these events. You can be a renegade, marketing "madman" or "madwoman" by going to these festivals armed with CDs and schmoozing with everyone in sight. Do not ever leave the opportunities of film (or TV) placement out of your music marketing plans! They can secure a lucrative future during any stage of your career. The Learning Annex website listed above has held courses specifically focused on pitching your work to Film and TV shows.

- www.starpolish.com - This is an oasis for Independent Artists, jam-packed with advice, resources, and an online community of support ranging from fellow Artists, Music Executives, Entertainment Attorneys, and many more. There are interviews done regularly on Independent Artists/Songwriters/Musicians like you.

- www.filmmusic.net - This is also a great resource to take advantage of. The Film Music Network gives you access to a database of Film and TV companies looking for specific types of music. It will deliver these listings regularly to your email box, or you can just access the site. This network is by membership only. For (roughly) $10.00/month, you can get these job listings, network with other members, and (most importantly) attend the monthly membership meetings/mixers that take place in numerous cities. These meetings normally cost around $15.00 each, but YOU GO FREE EACH MONTH if you are a member.

- www.licensemusic.com - This is another online music licensing company that follows the process of electronically distributing music to Film, TV, and other media companies in need of your sound for their campaigns. License Music will decide if they want your music in their catalog. The media companies will decide if they want to use it for their project(s).

- www.cdreview.com - This is another website that Independent Artists should check out. This company deals with product development/distribution specifically related to independent musical artists and CDs.

- www.websticker.com - You name it, and this website has

everything you need for promotional giveaways for your music or band, from bumper stickers, to decals, to labels and magnets. This is one way you can establish your logo identity or "brand" that will set you apart from the rest of the bunch in the public's eyes. These items make great gifts for fans and Industry alike. Many of you will find it easier than standing in line at a print shop and having to fuss through a paper catalog the size of a large stove. By the way, MAKE SURE YOU INCLUDE YOUR MUSIC WEBSITE ADDRESS ON EVERYTHING YOU PRINT!

- www.radio-locator.com - Got radio play? This is a complete database of ALL radio stations according to city, state, market, and format. It should save you a lot of time in your research of stations that might be appropriate for your style of music. It would be wise of you to visit this site and become familiar with what stations are out there. After all, most people do not know where to begin their searches, and this site is definitely the very best step you can take.

- www.calawyersforthearts.org - This is the website of the California Lawyers for the Arts organization. This is a cost-effective resource to tap into, as this firm deals exclusively with protecting the rights of the Artist. You might want to see if they can work with you, despite where you may live, in the event a music industry contract arrives for you that you should HAVE REVIEWED FIRST by an attorney.

- www.prepaidlegal.com - As a Musician or Artist, you must be very careful when it comes to understanding the details of the types of contracts you might presently be (or

89

hoping to be) entering into. Such examples include record deals, publishing or licensing deals, co-writing agreements, Film, TV, Internet, (and the list goes on). Unfortunately, a (potentially) risky situation can occur when Artists make the mistake of signing things they do not understand. Artists unfortunately (all-too-often) sign things they do not understand, simply because they CANNOT AFFORD AN ATTORNEY. After all, it can cost over $200.00 just to have one document reviewed! Before a company like this was invented, individuals with a lot of money were (generally) the only ones who had access to "their own Attorneys" when they needed them. The Attorneys this company has arrangements with will actually come to court with you if you are being sued. If it is in fact true that "the rest of society" can have the same type of legal protection and peace-of-mind (that the wealthy enjoy) at a microscopic percentage of what it would cost to hire someone privately, then this site might be "the answer" for many individuals, at least in terms of the number of "included" document/(in your case, "contract" reviews) each month that are included with the program.

- www.skratchmagazine.com - This online magazine caters to the indie rock, hardcore, garage, punk, and "skater scene." I include it here because the site has a very high readership. It could mean great exposure for you if you can get yourself/your music featured on it.

- www.openingbands.com - This is another online magazine published out of Chicago, and it has attracted a lot of attention, including from major record labels. There is quite a bit on this website, and the staff is comprised of

volunteers who are very passionate about music. It is
ALWAYS good business to introduce yourself, submit
your music, and correspond (even on a friendly basis).
Always think about getting to know these people (and
ALL Industry people) for the heck of it, while expecting
nothing back. You never know if they might suddenly
want to help you out, regardless of where you/your "Act"
are located.

- www.craigslist.org - You might not be aware that
Craigslist has entertainment sections that companies post
casting notices on, with tons of Film, TV, and other Media
Companies often requesting music for their projects. Each
has its own listing according to what city and state it is
located in. Entertainment Companies have often relied on
this FREE service when seeking talent. You can also
network with other Musicians and Artists all over the
country through message boards, as well as post your own
ads.

- www.musicares.org - This program was founded by the
National Academy of Recording Arts & Sciences
(NARAS). It provides assistance for musicians and artists
suffering from chemical dependency problems, as well as a
host of other issues. I urge you to become familiar with it if
you are in any kind of trouble and need assistance, or if you
just want to help out.

- www.snagajob.com - This is a website where you can
conveniently apply online for a part-time job at many of the
major retail restaurant franchises and shops you have
undoubtedly heard of. There are no "corporate" or "white-
collar" jobs here; just the "brick and mortar" ones. This is

the kind of resource that is great if you are new in town or you need to earn cash quickly, even if you have to settle for something that is below your educational level or skills. There is no shame in earning an honest dollar while you take the time to get your musical priorities in order.

*** The following websites are places to get your music licensed for Film, TV, and other media. These sites are worthy of your attention, but always use caution when dealing with ANY company. ***

- www.pumpaudio.com – This website connects Artists with Industry looking for music.

- www.youlicense.com – This website also connects Artists with Industry through digital licensing of songs.

- www.1212.com - This is the official website of the European Music Industry Directory. If you have thought about licensing your music overseas, or touring/getting a record deal overseas, you should find this website a highly useful resource.

- www.musiciansfriend.com – Discount musical instruments, accessories, duplication services, etc.

- www.nemoboston.com - Because I am a native of Boston, and because this festival takes place in Boston, I am including it in this report. The festival gives Artists and Musicians the opportunity to perform in front of the Industry folks (if your work is chosen) as well as the opportunity of attending the event and "networking," regardless of whether or not you perform there. This is a very large event and could serve as a decent gathering to promote yourself and your work.

- www.AirPlayDirect.com - Yes folks, once again, I need to remind you that we are in the digital age, and this could not possibly be a better time to be an Artist pursuing a Music Career. Do not let anyone feed you garbage about the Internet being too saturated. It is easier than ever (by light years, practically) to sell and promote your music, in a way that was unheard of just over a decade ago. But I want to talk for a moment about radio promotion. I have asked you before if it bothers you to spend a lot of time mailing out big, bulky, and expensive packages to radio stations, hoping they will play your songs. AirPlayDirect.com is a fine (and innovative) service that is unique, and could prove highly useful for Artists, Labels, AND Radio Stations, alike. This is NOT the same thing as a paid radio promotion company. For a very small fee per song, Artists' songs are uploaded via MP3 OR Wave File to an online database, enabling thousands of radio stations ALL OVER THE WORLD the opportunity of downloading broadcast-quality recordings of your songs (that are completely encrypted, with limits on the amount of downloads per station, and accessible ONLY to radio stations who sign up for the service). All Artists get their own private web page and log on screen to track ALL relevant statistics about number of downloads, "song popularity," etc.). You may also upload artwork, lyrics, and other useful statistics about your music. Complete details are at the airplaydirect.com URL. Using this service could save you some time AND money. Also, radio stations PAY NOTHING to download your songs, increasing the likelihood that they will take advantage of this service (while creating more room on their cluttered desks, which are over-piled with music CD's).

- www.smother.net - I include this ezine website because they claim to review EVERYTHING THEY RECEIVE. Although I do not always agree with the quote: "any publicity is good publicity," I will venture to say that, if this ezine can offer you some coverage for your music, it is probably worth your while. They cover just about every style of music out there. Check the site out and determine for yourself if it is right for you.

- www.musicdish.com & www.mi2n.com - Edgy, innovative, and just plain cool are some descriptions that come to mind as I describe these two websites. The first site (www.musicdish.com) is a pure and cutting-edge authority on the world of modern music. The second site (www.mi2n.com) has a truly impressive and unique FREE service that blesses Artists and Musicians with the ability to submit their own Press Releases through their website, after which the company distributes the Press Releases electronically to many key sources that can potentially help in the advancement of their music careers. We all should know by now that Press is the most important element in catapulting a music career because, without it, nothing happens!

- www.productionhub.com - This website saved me an unbelievable amount of time. I have never found anything quite like this website/company (or as convenient as this website) anywhere on the Internet, and I am sure you will not either. This is (yet another) entirely FREE and convenient service that is PERFECT for Artists and Musicians. I have used it myself, and received first-class treatment all the way. The Sole Purpose of productionhub.com is to connect, or "match," you with the appropriate type of Production Company, based on the specific kind of production you want to create. If you need a music video, commercial, or any other production you can think of, simply enter your information along with the type of project you have in mind and, within a day (or just a few days more), you will start to receive emails from companies who specialize in your particular work, along with price quotes. Again, I saved a lot of time using productionhub.com, and you will too. Without a service like this, it is tough to know where to begin if your feet are not wet yet.

■ www.budgetvideo.com – This company has every type of camera available for rental, and is particularly useful for a music video done "on a budget."

■ ***The following websites are the "holy 3" Performance Rights Organizations. There is a "4th" site for Canadian Performance Rights. Their specific function is to collect royalties for you (on your behalf) for the use of your music in various media, and you should join one of them if you want to see any dollar signs for the use of your work in geographic areas you are otherwise unable to collect from. All have their advantages and disadvantages, yet the decision of which one to join is up to you. They all offer various opportunities (on occasion) to network and perform. You can also get discounts on things like insurance (health/dental), as well as discounts on equipment. You MUST join one of these organizations as a "Publishing Company" to collect royalties for various uses of your music in the media. However, it does not matter whether or not the name you already chose for your record company has been taken or not ("outside of" these organizations). You will join under your personal name, or if you have a great idea for a Publishing Company name, any of these royalty collection agencies will check for the use of the name by another member, and if nobody else is using the name, you can sign up under the name.

- www.ascap.com - American Society of Composers, Authors, and Publishers
- www.bmi.com - Broadcast Music, Inc.
- www.sesac.com - Performing Rights Organization for Songwriters and Publishers
- www.socan.ca - Society of Composers, Authors & Music Publishers of Canada (SOCAN) – (Toronto, Ontario) – (800) 55-SOCAN

- www.radiocountry.org - This is the official site of the annual Nashville Music Festival. This is a regularly held, 3-day extravaganza for Artists and Bands to connect with Industry folks, and vice-versa. Going to this site and learning how you might perform at this festival (along with finding out the details of the many other benefits/resources the festival has to offer) could only serve you. Many other festivals are listed on this website, too.

I realize many of you are located around the world. In fact, this is my hope because I want to include a set of Songwriting and Music Business Organizations that are specific to areas around the entire globe. It is very wise to join an organization. It is a great way to network, make contacts, exchange creative ideas/collaborate, or just make friends that share the same passion for music. You can even become active in the actual decision-making processes of the organization(s) by inquiring. You might stumble upon a lead that (for all you know) could end up affecting the future of your music career in a very beneficial/substantial way … Please review the following, according to wear you live. If a website address was not available, I have (attempted) to provide an email address and/or phone number to the organization. (Please also note that, in addition to the types of organizations just mentioned, I also want to readdress the issue of music video streaming and video production by including a list of sites that specialize in this for Independent Artists/bands. These video sites are labeled as such, so as not to confuse them with the Songwriting and Networking organizations also listed).

- www.anywho.com – (U.S.A.) Nationwide "people finder."

- www.songwritersresourcenetwork.com – Songwriting resources and organizations across the entire U.S. continent and abroad.

- www.songwriteruniverse.com – Songwriting resources, organizations, publishers, record labels, clubs, publications, producers, and studios galore.

- www.songwritersdirectory.com – A nationwide database for songwriters and associations.
- www.tsamusic.com – Tim Sweeney's official website, and home of Music Strategies.
- Alabama Songwriter's Guild – (256) 352-4873
- www.aimp.org - Association of Independent Music Publishers – New York, NY – (212) 758-6157
- www.bostonsongwriters.org - The Boston Songwriters Workshop
- www.afm.org – American Federation of Musicians - This is the union for musicians that offers pension programs for live performances, musician referrals, performance venue referrals, and other production resources, including recording studios with discounted rates, and resources for shooting music videos. There are required dues to join, and there are different chapters of the AFM according to what city and state you happen to live in.

- www.canadacouncil.ca - Canada Council for the Arts
- www.juno-awards.ca - Canada Academy of Recording Arts & Sciences
- www.ccma.org - Canada Country Music Association (CCMA)
- www.cmrra.ca - Canadian Musical Reproduction Rights Agency, Ltd.
- www.under.org/cpcc - Center for the Promotion of Contemporary Composers (Texas)
- http://COSA4U.tripod.com - Central Oregon Songwriters Association
- www.music.org - The College Music Society (Montana)
- http://coloradomusic.org - Colorado Music Association

- Composers Guild (Utah) – (801) 451-2275
- www.isound.com – A complete online music marketing suite for independent musicians, songwriters, and bands, with many FREE features to access.
- www.insound.com – Vinyl Artists are featured here
- www.ctsongs.com - Connecticut Songwriters Association
- Country Music Association of Texas – (254) 938-2454
- www.cmshowcase.org - Country Music Showcase International, Inc. (based out of Iowa).
- www.thefield.org - The Field (New York, NY)
- www.folk.org - The Folk Alliance (North American Folk Music and Dance Alliance) – (Washington, DC)
- www.fwsa.com - Fort Worth Songwriters Association (Texas)
- www.muchmusic.com - Video Streaming
- www.sputnik7.com - Video Streaming
- www.gmia.org - Georgia Music Industry Association, Inc.
- www.gospelmusic.org - Gospel Music Association (Nashville, TN)
- www.angelfire.com/music/ncgcsg - Gospel/Christian Songwriters Group
- www.songwriters-guild.com - The Guild of International Songwriters & Composers (England)
- www.songwriter.co.uk - International Songwriters Association, Ltd. (England)
- www.isgorlando.org - International Songwriters Guild – (407) 851-5328 – (Orlando, FL)
- www.jpfolks.com - Just Plain Folks Music Organization (IN)

- www.lamn.com - Los Angeles Music Network (Universal City, CA)

- www.songwriteruniverse.com/kentuckysa.html - Songwriter Associations for Kentucky, Louisiana, Maine, Maryland, and Massachusetts
- www.manitobamusic.com - Manitoba Music Industry Association (Canada)
- www.meetthecomposer.org - Meet the Composer (New York, NY)
- www.memphissongwriters.org - Memphis Songwriters Association (Memphis, TN)
- www.mnsongwriters.org - Minnesota Association of Songwriters
- www.musicianscontact.com - Musicians Contact (regular listings of PAYING JOBS for musicians and artists)
- www.nashvillesongwriters.com - Nashville Songwriters Association International (NSAI)
- www.music-usa.org/nacusa - The National Association of Composers/USA (NACUSA)
- www.westcoastsongwriters.org – West Coast Songwriters, formerly the Northern California Songwriters Association – (800) FORSONG
- www.outmusic.com - OutMusic (gay & lesbian)
- Pacific Northwest Songwriters Association - (Seattle, WA) – (206) 824-1568
- www.pasamusic.org - Philadelphia Area Songwriters Alliance
- www.portlandsongwriters.org - Portland Songwriters Association (OR)
- www.risongwriters.com - Rhode Island Songwriters Association (RISA)

- www.sdsongwriters.org - San Diego Songwriters Guild – (CA)
- www.sffmc.org - San Francisco Folk Music Club

- www.sodrac.com - Sodrac, Inc. – (Canada) – Management of Rights of Artists
- The Songwriters Advocate (TSA) – (Rochester, NY) – (716) 266-0679
- www.songwriterscritique.com - Songwriters and Poets Critique (Columbus, OH)
- www.saw.org - Songwriters Association of Washington (Washington, DC)
- www.songwritersguild.com - The Songwriters Guild of America (SGA) –(New York, NY)
- www.oklahomasongwriters.com - Oklahoma Songwriters & Composers Association (O.S.C.A)
- www.songwritersofwisconsin.org - Songwriters of Wisconsin International – (Neenah, WI) – (920) 725-1609
- www.SongwritersResourceNetwork.com - Songwriters Resource Network – (Portland, OR)
- www.scmatx.org - Southwest Celtic Music Association – (Dallas, TX)
- www.spars.com - SPARS (Society of Professional Audio Recording Services) – (Memphis, TN)
- www.tnsai.com - The Tennessee Songwriters Association International – (Hendersonville, TN)
- www.governor.state.tx.us/music - Texas Music Office - (Austin, TX)
- www.victorymusic.org - Victory Music – (Tacoma, WA)
- www.wamadc.com - Washington Area Music Association – (Washington, DC)

- www.womeninmusic.org - Women in Music – (New York, NY)

25.) ELECTRONIC PRESS RELEASES

- www.cpwire.com - Collegiate Presswire
- www.prweb.com - PRWeb
- www.eworldwire.com - EWORLDWIRE
- www.internetnewsbureau.com - Internet News Bureau
- www.netpost.com - Net Post
- www.urlwire.com - url launch/website announcement service
- www.xpresspress.com - Xpress Press
- www.marketwire.com - Market Wire
- www.newstarget.com - News Target

26.) ONLINE DIGITAL INDEPENDENT MUSIC WEBSITES

- www.emusic.com
- www.garageband.com
- www.epitonic.com

Cheers, this is the END of the book, and it is dedicated to your new BEGINNING. Wishing you MAXIMUM success with your work!

Paul S. Alexander

NOTES